Heaven:
it's not the end of the world

Heaven:
it's not the end of the world

David Lawrence

Scripture Union, 207–209 Queensway, Bletchley MK2 2EB
Email: info@scriptureunion.org.uk
Website: www.scriptureunion.org.uk

We are an international Christian charity working with churches in
more than 130 countries providing resources to bring the good news
about Jesus Christ to children, young people and families – and to
encourage them to develop spiritually through the Bible and prayer.

As well as our network of volunteers, staff and associates who run
holidays, church-based events and school Christian groups, we
produce a wide range of publications and support those who use our
resources through training programmes.

First published 1995
Reprinted 2002

ISBN 0 86201 950 8

British Library Cataloguing-in-Publication Data
A catalogue record for this book is available from the British
Library.

Cover design and illustration by Grax Design Consultants.

Phototypeset by Servis Filmsetting Ltd, Manchester.
Printed and bound in Great Britain by CPD Wales, Ebbw Vale

This book is dedicated to Sue Stringer
who has already passed into Paradise
where she joyfully dances in the presence of Jesus.
Eternally secure in the Father's love
she patiently awaits the day
when she will return with Jesus to the renewed earth.
Then she will receive her resurrection body
and be reunited with those who love her
and love her Lord.

I should like to thank the following people who in
some way encouraged or advised me as I
wrote this book

My ever-encouraging wife, Myrtle

Alison Barr for her careful and patient work as editor

Tony Billinghurst, Nick Mercer and Tony Hobbs for
their many helpful comments on the manuscript

Nancy Beard for providing me with solitude, coffee
and Welsh cakes while writing

CONTENTS

NB As you will see from the above, Part 1 of this book provides a broad biblical basis for the theme of creation renewed. Part 2 deals in more detail with what life on the new earth may be like. Some readers may prefer to read the more descriptive Part 2 before returning to the Bible base of Part 1. In either case, Part 3 – the contemporary implications of belief in a renewed earth – is best left to the end!

PREFACE

On September 11th 2001, the angel of sudden and violent death, for so long an inhabitant of the 'two thirds world', dared to call in on the West and shocked us with his cruelty.

Hours after terrorist hijackers flew civilian aeroplanes into the twin towers of the World Trade Centre in New York and the Pentagon in Washington, Christian commentators – and the non-Christian media – were describing the events in apocalyptic, end-of-the-world language.

When the dust had settled (but long before all the bodies were recovered) some Christian commentators were trying to place this tragedy – and the so-called 'war on terrorism' which it precipitated – in a scheme of events which would herald (so they claimed) the return of Jesus Christ.

Did 'armaggedon' start on September 11th 2001? Or how about the 'great tribulation'? Is 'the antichrist' finally showing himself? And surely Israel's role cannot be purely incidental?

In other words questions were asked about God's timetable for the 'end-times' and where (if at all) the fall of the Twin Towers figures in it.

Now these questions are understandable – indeed, for the Church to fail to wrestle theologically with events of such gravity would be an abdication of responsibility. However, in this book I want to push the questions beyond the 'traditional' end-of-the-world issues and ask a bigger – and to my mind more important – question: when armaggedon has happened, when the tribulation has occurred, when we know for sure whether or not there is a rapture (and if there is who goes where when!), when the Lord Jesus has returned, and when pre-, post-, or a-millennialists know who is right – WHAT THEN?

I have many books on my shelves dealing with the 'end-times'. Page after page on 'the signs of the times', the antichrist, the millennium, the great tribulation and the rapture (or not!). The return of Jesus Christ is expounded in great detail, and the judgement of the living and the dead usually receives good coverage too. Then – almost as an afterthought – the glorious new age gets a chapter at best or, more usually, a few vague, concluding paragraphs.

I have always found it strange and mildly frustrating that so much attention is lavished on the stepping-stones across the stream and so little interest shown in what God has laid in store on the far bank. Or, to use a more biblical metaphor, the 'end-time' signs Paul describes as merely 'labour pains' (Romans 8:22) often appear to be of more interest than the new creation which is to be born!

This emphasis undoubtedly serves to heighten our fascination with God's appointed means to the end, but leaves our inner selves uninspired by what the future holds for us. It is my conviction that what keeps us going when the going gets tough is neither a vision of the rapture, nor a belief in one of the several views on the millennium, but rather the hope that one day God will put it all right. One day life, the universe and everything will not be like this – it will be radically, unimaginably better. The earth itself will be renewed, righteous humanity will be resurrected, and life on our planet will be as God originally intended – joyful, glorious and saturated with a sense of his presence in every part.

Therefore, I have resolved to write this book with the major focus being on the age to come – the great future that God has promised on the renewed earth as the inheritance for all who are 'saved by faith'.

If only we could spend more time reflecting on and making plain this wonderful vision of our eternal destiny, and less time haggling over the means by which God may bring it about, then perhaps the church could once again offer real hope for the future to people who in this age are struggling with a sense of meaninglessness.

When the towers fall, people do not want theological debate, or a timetable of disasters; they want hope that God has planned – indeed promised – that something beautiful will arise out of the ashes of this world's demise. People who are not moved by theological millennial niceties may well be moved by a biblical picture of creation redeemed. So let's stop arguing about the nature, strength and frequency of the labour pains and start celebrating what is to be born!

David Lawrence

PART 1

BIBLICAL FOUNDATIONS FOR A NEW EARTH

'We believe . . . that God created the earth, entrusting its care to man, and that he will one day re-create it, when he makes "the new heaven and the new earth".'

John Stott

'Very often people have come to the New Testament with the presumption that "going to heaven when you die" is the implicit point of it all . . . They acquire this viewpoint from somewhere, but not from the New Testament!'

Tom Wright

Chapter 1

WHERE ON EARTH ARE WE GOING?

'I feel a bit ashamed to admit it but I reckon heaven is going to be boring.'

'Really?' I hadn't expected such a frank confession from a close Christian friend.

'Yes. I mean, what will there be to do? I know the prospect of being with Jesus and worshipping him for ever should be enough, but . . .' She tailed off, uncertain how to voice her feelings. However, her comments had already confirmed what I had begun to suspect: that for most Christians heaven is a bit like Timbuktu; everyone has heard of it but very few people have a clear idea of where it is or what it would be like to live there!

For many people, 'heaven' conjures up images of crowds of happy winged spirits, miraculously balancing various sizes of crowns on their heads whilst eternally floating down gold-paved streets strumming the Hallelujah Chorus on their standard-issue harps!

To picture heaven in this way, as a final Great Escape from all that hurts and harms, a solo-flight of the spirit into the arms of a loving God, is a beautiful thought and, it must be said, a very comforting one for people whose lives in the here and now are full of pain and suffering. The question that must be asked, however, is not whether these images of heaven are beautiful and comforting (since they undoubtedly are) but whether they are true!

Does the Bible really lead us to expect eternity to be an ecstatic spiritual experience as we worship around the throne of God? Are we to spend the age to come as happy spirits basking in a 'realm of light' out there beyond the blue? Certainly this view finds support in many a hymn book. Take this offering from Anne Shepherd as an example:

> Around the throne of God in heaven
> > Thousands of children stand.
> Children whose sins are all forgiven,
> > A holy, happy band.
>
> In flowing robes of spotless white
> > See every one arrayed,
> Dwelling in everlasting light
> > And joys that never fade.

But have the hymn writers and those who peddle the popular notion of heaven got it right? Certain other biblical doctrines do not appear to sit very comfortably with these visions of children dressed in flowing robes, eternally standing in the everlasting light of God's throne. Two doctrines in particular strike a discordant note.

First, what are we to make of physical resurrection? Why do we need a new human body to enjoy 'heavenly' bliss? Surely there is an inconsistency here. Does the very promise of *physical* resurrection not imply a more *physical* eternity than traditional views of heaven would allow?

Second, if heaven is to be our home, what are we to make of God's explicit promise to create 'new heavens *and a new earth*' where he himself will live with humanity,[1] and of the implied intention to renew *all* things (all, presumably, including the earth) at the return of Jesus?[2]

Once we begin to wrestle with these biblical promises of *earthly* renewal and re-creation, a host of related questions jostle for our attention. If the earth is to be renewed, what will the new earth be like? Will it bear any relation to this earth? Who (if anyone) will live on it? Will it have animal and plant life? And how does the existence of a new earth affect our understanding of heaven as our eternal home?

Interesting questions to be sure, but the biblical doctrine of a re-created earth, as well as challenging some of our assumptions about our future heavenly existence, will also make us rethink some of our attitudes to our present earthly one.

Seeing God's ultimate plan for us as being 'heavenly' and 'spiritual' has led us to imagine that spiritual things are God's chief concern. If a spiritual heaven is God's greatest good for us, then the earth and our physical existence on it must be somehow 'second best'. Consequently, many Christians hold the view that the only reason God created the earth was to give people somewhere to live whilst they decide whether or not to follow Jesus! Once everyone has had the chance to make up their minds on that one vital issue, God is going to whisk his people from the earth to a place of eternal spiritual security (called 'heaven') whilst the earth, having fulfilled its function, is discarded and burnt up.

In this traditional view the earth has no status in itself other than as a kind of 'space station' for God's salvation mission. What we do to it and how we treat it are largely irrelevant since it's destined for the bonfire anyway!

However, if one believes that God owns and loves *all* of his creation and that one day he will renew it *all* in his love, then one's whole perspective on the earth and its inhabitants changes. The question of the earth and its future becomes vital, not only to our future hope and expectation but also to the way we live as God's people *now*.

It is my firm belief that the future God has planned for us will *not* be 'heavenly' (in the usual way of understanding the term) nor will it be in the least boring! Theologian Tom Wright observes, 'Very often people have come to the New Testament with the presumption that "going to heaven when you die" is the implicit point of it all . . . They acquire that viewpoint from somewhere, but not from the New Testament!'[3]

Rather, as I shall seek to show, the whole Bible leads us to expect a glorious renewal of life on earth, so that the age to come will be an endlessly thrilling adventure of living with God on the new earth. With his presence pervading every act, we shall be more fully human than we have ever been, liberated from sin, death and all that hurts or harms. In the well-known words of Martin Luther King, we shall be 'free at last, free at last! Thank God Almighty, we'll be free at last!'

It is an awe-inspiring hope that we have, and this book seeks to explore some of the biblical background that underpins this hope and to unpack some of the exciting possibilities of what life on the new earth might be like. This will be new territory for many readers, and perhaps a health warning might be in order before going any further.

In the first two chapters of the book I shall survey the Old and New Testaments to see whether the 'traditional' view of heaven is really to be found there. Did the Old Testament Israelites look forward to heaven in the same way that we do? Did John, Peter and Paul anticipate 'going to heaven' as the climax to life on earth and, more importantly, did Jesus? As we look at many familiar (and some less familiar) texts, a radical picture will begin to emerge of a far more 'earthly' future hope than we have ever understood. Inevitably, perhaps, we shall initially raise more questions than answers, but please read on. As the book unfolds I am sure you will find that questions posed by early chapters are answered in later ones; and I hope you will find the pieces gradually fitting together to give you a clear understanding of the new earth that God has already prepared in his heart for those who love him.

THE OLD TESTAMENT VIEW

In the beginning . . .
Let's begin our search at the very beginning, Genesis chapter 1.

'In the beginning God created the heavens and the earth.'[4] The phrase 'the heavens and the earth' used here in Genesis is simply a way of saying 'everything'. Every part of the cosmos exists only because God willed it to be there. Indeed, the whole point of Genesis 1 is to prove that God is Creator, owner and sustainer of everything. In a world of apparent chaos and disorder, the highly structured Hebrew of Genesis 1 (a structure that is largely lost in the English translations) reassures us that there is plan and purpose to the universe, the world and our very existence as humans in it.

Having started with this big picture of God's cosmic owner-ship, Genesis 1 deals in detail with just one small part of 'every-thing', namely the great care which God took to produce a beautiful and fruitful planet called 'earth'. Whether you believe that God did this in six twenty-four-hour days or whether you favour a less literal interpretation of a 'day' is, to my mind, less important than grasping the incredible love and attention which God lavished on creating the earth. God's pleasure in his work is underlined by the frequent descriptions of his 'daily' inspections and pronouncements that it was good. Vegetation and fruit made God happy.[5] He looked at fish, birds, animals and all living creatures and found delight in what he saw.[6]

We are surely forced to conclude that even if God had not placed humanity on the planet it would have pleased and delighted him each time he looked at it. It bore the 'fingerprints' of his creative skills and was full of life, colour and limitless potential. But how to develop that potential? Who would do the gardening in this rich Paradise that had been spoken into being? Who would discover and develop the vast deposits of minerals and precious stones to further enhance and beautify the planet and the lives of the creatures who lived on it? Who would care for the animals and who would enjoy the earth's fruitfulness? God could have kept it to himself but hoarding is not in God's character!

God said, 'Let us make humankind in our image, accord-ing to our likeness; and let them have dominion over the fish of the sea, and over the birds of the air, and over the cattle, and over all the wild animals of the earth, and over every creeping thing that creeps upon the earth.' So God created humankind . . .[7]

It is clear that here at the beginning humans and the created order *belonged together*, and therefore we could only fulfil our potential and reach our destiny if we functioned as a part of the rest of creation. God did not place us here as a kind of endurance test to see if we could cope with spiders, thunderstorms and one another, with those who pass the test being beamed up 'to heaven'! From Genesis 1 it appears that the earth was meant to be our home for ever and ever, and God placed us on it because this is where we belong – at the heart of his beloved creation, caring for it and developing its potential.

The workers revolt

This wonderful picture of God and man working in partnership, with humanity acting as willing and obedient overseers of creation, is soon shattered. The story of the Fall[8] is one of tragedy on a cosmic scale. Humanity decided that they knew better than God and, instead of remaining in submissive partnership with him, gave in to the temptation to take responsibility for life into their own hands. They disobeyed one of the very few orders they had been given and, in just one act of disobedience, fractured the vital relationship between God and his creation. Humanity, who were to be the supply-line of God's loving care for the rest of the earth's inhabitants, decided to do their own thing. Life on earth has never fully recovered from that decision.

The implications were vast. Human relationships, so vital if men and women were to co-operate in their role of stewarding creation, became filled with suspicion, jealousy and hatred. The very fabric of earth was somehow to mirror man's rebellion so that land which had previously been fertile became barren. The act of working the land, once a pleasure, was now to become back-breaking laborious toil. Human beings, who were to have lived for ever on the earth, were now to die and return to the dust from which they were formed. And, most terribly of all, mankind's intimacy with God was lost. The workforce of creation was now running wild, making up its own rules and trying to order life without reference to the boss.

Creation condemned

Not surprisingly, things went from bad to worse and it was not long before God had seen enough. The pain of his beautiful

earth being exploited and his beloved humanity tearing themselves to bits was too much, and he regretted the days of
creation. Two of the most terrible verses in the Bible let us in on
God's private grief.

> The Lord saw that the wickedness of humankind was great
> in the earth, and that every inclination of the thoughts of
> their hearts was only evil continually. And the Lord was
> sorry that he had made humankind on the earth, and it
> grieved him to his heart. So the Lord said, 'I will blot out
> from the earth the human beings I have created – people
> together with animals and creeping things and birds of the
> air, for I am sorry that I have made them.'[9]

The depth of hurt and regret revealed in God's heart once again
underlines just how much he loved the earth that he had created
and just how far it had fallen from being what he intended it to
be. The chapter goes on:

> And God said . . . 'I have determined to make an end of
> all flesh, for the earth is filled with violence because of
> them; now I am going to destroy them along with the
> earth.'[10]

This is terrible but also, from our perspective, of some interest
because God did *not* literally destroy the earth. Rather, in an act
of divine judgement, he *cleansed* the earth by sending a flood
that destroyed not the very fabric of creation itself but the evil
which had conspired to destroy it. It is quite clear that God's
desire was still to see his earth filled with the human race which
he so loved because, having judged and destroyed human
wickedness, he took the risk of allowing just one family to start
life *on earth* again.

Just one good man (Noah), whose goodness protected his
family by securing them 'boarding passes' for the ark, was
chosen to form the nucleus of the new generation of God-
obeying earth-stewards.

Once again we find humanity re-commissioned to 'be fruit-ful and multiply, and fill the earth'. Humankind had been delivered through the flood to fulfil its earthbound destiny, and God made promises to Noah and his family (and, interestingly, to the animal kingdom) that never again would such a judge-ment fall.[11]

Nevertheless, it would be wrong to see this cleansed earth as *completely* renewed. A wicked society had been washed away in the sea of God's righteous anger but evil itself had not been destroyed. Even as God repeats the promises and commands given in Genesis 1, we see that the effects of the Fall are still to be taken into account; wicked people have been justly destroyed but creation itself is still under the influence of the presence of evil.

So instead of humanity, as it were, ruling by love, they were now to rule the animals by 'fear and dread';[12] instead of being able to eat only the plants for food,[13] God makes concession to the continuing presence of death in the animal kingdom by allowing humans to eat the flesh of dead animals. Life on earth is cleansed and renewed but not yet 'saved' from the conse-quences of the presence of evil.

God's new garden

Sadly, but inevitably, it was not long before evil once again began to mar and destroy humanity's ability to care for the earth. Having promised not to destroy the earth and its inhab-itants by flood, what would God do? He now instituted the next phase of his plan. If humanity at large was incapable of estab-lishing his rule of righteousness on the earth, then he would call into being a particular group of people with whom he would live in close relationship. These people would become his special, distinctive nation and would begin to demonstrate to onlooking nations just how God wanted life on earth to 'work'.

God needed a starting point and he chose just one man to begin this great project of establishing a holy nation on the earth. His name? Abram. His commission? To go to a new land in which, God said, 'I will make of you a great nation, and I will bless you, and make your name great, so that you will be a bless-ing . . . in you all the families of the earth shall be blessed.'[14] Once again we see that God's programme for humanity was blessing, and blessing *on the earth*.

Abram faithfully responded to God's challenge and travelled to the land of Canaan. As he gazed over its dusty hills and won-dered whether this could really be the place of God's choosing (after all, the Canaanites were still living there), God 'appeared to Abram and said, "To your offspring I will give this land".'

Note that God's people needed a land in which to reach their destiny as a holy nation. As in the days of Noah, God could have dematerialized righteous humanity to a never-never land called heaven but, once again, his passion for his creation in its totality (not simply in its humanity) led him to continue to pursue a policy of harmonizing life on earth in all of its differ-ent guises – animal, plant and human.

To cut a long – and well-known – story short, the promise that God made to Abram eventually came true. A new nation, led by God through Moses, arrived at the borders of the prom-ised land. Under Joshua this nation moved into Canaan, and God worked and fought for them to redeem the land from the occupying tribes. When Canaan's conquest was nearly com-plete the people settled into tribes and family groups. Towns were built, and the nation began to attempt to order life in the way that God wanted.

To guide them God gave them many laws. It is interesting to note that these laws cover all aspects of life – the practical (eg 'When you build a new house, you shall make a parapet for your roof; otherwise you might have bloodguilt on your house, if anyone should fall from it'[15]), the social (eg 'You shall not watch your neighbour's ox or sheep straying away and ignore them; you shall take them back to their owner'[16]) and the 'religious' (eg 'You must not sacrifice to the Lord your God an ox or a sheep that has a defect . . . for that is abhorrent to the Lord your God'[17]).

These laws provided an invaluable code, ensuring that this new nation, so central to God's purposes, truly reflected his loving and righteous character to the surrounding nations. When people looked at Israel they should see the character of God being fleshed out before them, not only in their acts of worship but in the way they treated one another, and even in the way they built their houses and respected one another's property!

However, there was one other area covered by the laws given to Israel: God instructed people how to serve him within the boundaries of Canaan as *stewards of his prized creation*, by giving laws that reflected his concern for the animal kingdom and the 'heath' of the very soil itself. For example, they were told, 'If you come on a bird's nest, in any tree or on the ground, with fledglings or eggs, with the mother sitting on the fledglings or on the eggs, you shall not take the mother with the young. Let the mother go . . . in order that it may go well with you and you may live long.'[18] Each bird was important to God and he cared how they were treated.

The land was to be used with care and respect and not over-farmed or exploited: 'Six years you shall sow your field, and six years you shall prune your vineyard, and gather in their yield; but in the seventh year there shall be a sabbath of complete rest for the land'.[19] Here again we see God's intention to teach human beings how to find fulfilment by living in harmony and sympathy with creation.

When is a nation not a nation?

It cannot be overestimated how important it was to Israel to be custodians of God's land. Chris Wright observes, 'A fundamental constituent of [God's promises to Abram] . . . is that God would give Abram and his descendants *a land*. That land becomes one of the most prominent features of the entire sequel of the Old Testament story . . . The overarching theme of the great history of the Pentateuch, on through the books of Joshua and Judges and up to the establishing of the territorial limits of the kingdom of David, is the promise and possession of the land.'[20] This theme continues beyond Old Testament times right down to present day Judaism.

The importance of the land to Israel's nationhood is demonstrated most powerfully when judgement comes in the form of exile from the land. Sitting by the rivers of Babylon, the people should still have been capable of seeing themselves as a nation. They were still able to relate to one another as God wanted and still able to sing songs of praise to God. Yet all this meant nothing to them because, they said, 'How could we sing the Lord's song *in a foreign land*?'[21] Being God's people was only possible in its fullest sense when they were rooted in the land that God had promised them with access to the temple as the focus for their worship. Only in Canaan could they give full expression to their nationhood. A kind of spiritual relationship with God in a foreign land was not their destiny and could not be cause for celebration. To be God's people they needed the terra firma of Canaan and access to the holy city, Jerusalem, where God dwelt in the temple. Trying to live for God in Babylon was not the point of their existence. They had been called into being in order to establish a righteous, God-honouring nation in Canaan and nothing less than that would do.

Back to the land

As prisoners in a foreign country, who could give the exiled people of God hope? Had God cut them off, or was there a chance that his promises to Abram could, even at this lowest point in their fortunes, be restored?

Enter the prophets, men inspired and commissioned by God to reveal to Israel what was on God's heart for them. Some spoke out before the exile, some during it and some after the survivors had returned to Canaan. Each prophet was raised up by God to bring his word to his people at a particular point in their history. Different prophets therefore addressed different issues within the life of Israel and Judah. There is one theme, however, which recurs in many of the prophets' messages – that of restoration *to* the land and restoration *of* the land.

The prophet Ezekiel, who prophesied during the years of Israel's exile, foretells a day when, God says, 'I will restore the fortunes of Jacob, and have mercy on the whole house of Israel; and I will be jealous for my holy name . . . Then they shall know that I am the Lord their God because I sent them into exile among the nations, and then gathered them into their own land. I will leave none of them behind . . .'[22]

Joel, thought by many to be one of the earliest of the Old Testament prophetic books, warned Israel of impending disaster unless they repented; but he also saw beyond judgement to a time when Israel would be restored to harmony with the promised land. The picture of God's people, living in harmony with the rest of his creation and enjoying its fruitfulness, is beautiful and bears repeating here in full.

> Then the Lord became jealous for his land [*note!*] and
>   had pity on his people.
> In response to his people the Lord said:
> I am sending you grain, wine, and oil, and you will be
>   satisfied;
> and I will no more make you a mockery among the
>   nations . . .
>
> Do not fear, O soil [*note!*]; be glad and rejoice, for the
>   Lord has done great things! ·
> Do not fear, you animals of the field, for the pastures of
>   the wilderness are green;
> the tree bears its fruit, the fig tree and vine give their full
>   yield.
>
> O children of Zion, be glad and rejoice in the Lord your
>   God;
> for he has given the early rain for your vindication, he
>   has poured down for you abundant rain, the early
>   and the later rain, as before.
> The threshing floor shall be full of grain, the vats shall
>   overflow with wine and oil.
>
> I will repay you for the years that the swarming locust
>   has eaten,

> the hopper, the destroyer, and the cutter, my great army,
>   which I sent against you.
>
> You shall eat in plenty and be satisfied, and praise the
>   name of the Lord your God, who has dealt
>   wondrously with you . . .
> You shall know that I am in the midst of Israel, and that
>   I, the Lord, am your God and there is no other.[23]

Through Joel's words, God promised the future reunion of land (soil), animals and people in harmonious and fruitful relationship. Indeed, nearly all of the Old Testament prophets, even those who foretold in graphic detail the judgements that would overtake faithless Israel, communicated a visionary hope for future restoration expressed in similar earthly terms. From Isaiah's picture of the wolf living with the lamb and the leopard lying down with the kid, through Amos' rebuilt ruined cities and Micah's swords being formed into ploughshares, to Malachi's fruitful 'land of delight',[24] Israel's future hope was undeniably earthbound. Their future was inextricably linked with the future of God's creation, and any notion of a 'spiritual' heaven which would replace the splendours of creation was notable by its absence!

If, therefore, you were to ask an Old Testament Israelite what the future held, he would have expressed himself in purely physical terms. Certainly the individual would have believed that after death his soul would enter the 'world of the dead',[25] but that would not have been the centre pole of his future hope. His hope for the future – even though he might not be alive to see it himself – would be that God would restore the nation of Israel to their land, that the land itself would become unusually fruitful, that under the rulership of God's anointed King life on the earth would become just and peaceful, and that even the animals in the land would live in harmony with one another. From beginning to end, then, we are beginning to see that the Old Testament views the destiny of humanity as being inextricably linked with life *on the earth*.

But what about heaven?

This belief system and end-time hope of the holy nation restored to its land was the one that Jesus would have been born into, and yet it is so different to the end-time hope of heaven that we live with. Where did our hope come from? Did Jesus refute the Old Testament hope of creation restored and interpret the descriptive language of the prophets as merely symbolic of some as yet unknown age to come? Is the Old Testament providing merely a shadowy picture of the reality of heaven and, if so, does the New Testament blow away any of the fog and attempt to redefine heaven for us in terms spiritual and ethereal? These questions lead us into the next chapter.

NOTES ON CHAPTER 1

1   Isaiah 66:22; 2 Peter 3:13; Revelation 21:1–5.
2   Matthew 19:28.
3   N T Wright, Drew lecture, 1993, used with permission.
4   Genesis 1:1 (NIV).
5   Genesis 1:12.
6   Genesis 1:21,25.
7   Genesis 1:26,27.
8   See Genesis 3.
9   Genesis 6:5–7.
10 Genesis 6:13.
11 Genesis 9:8–17.
12 Genesis 9:2.
13 Genesis 1:29.
14 Genesis 12:2.
15 Deuteronomy 22:8.
16 Deuteronomy 22:1.
17 Deuteronomy 17:1.
18 Deuteronomy 22:6.
19 Leviticus 25:3–4.
20 C J H Wright, *Living as the people of God*, Inter-Varsity Press, 1984.

21 Psalm 137:4.
22 Ezekiel 39:25,28.
23 Joel 2:18–27.
24 Isaiah 11; Amos 9; Micah 4; Malachi 3:11,12.
25 See chapter four.

Chapter 2

THE RENEWAL OF ALL THINGS

JESUS' VIEW

Jesus is the focal point of all scripture so let's begin our search of the New Testament with an examination of his end-time teaching.

New developments

The world of Jesus' day had clearly moved on in the 400 years since the close of the Old Testament. The ideas of the Greek philosopher Plato (428–347 BC), that the higher, spiritual world was in fact the 'real' world and that "once released from its imprisonment in the body, the spirit . . . became stronger and more powerful", rising up to enjoy "its ultimate home in the transcendent, celestial realm of Platonic ideas"[1] had made an impact on people's expectations of the age to come, making it more 'spiritual' and less 'physical'.

Influenced by Plato's ideas, the influential Jewish thinker Philo of Alexandria (20 BC–AD 45) taught that "since the soul belongs to the spiritual world, life in the body is nothing but a brief, often unfortunate, episode" and that after death the soul assumes a "higher existence immortal and incorporeal". In this era, as Greek thinking took a hold, many in Israel lost the vision for a restored earthly identity and accepted a view based on Plato's individualised, spiritual teaching.

Whilst indeed *some* Jews of Jesus' days appear to have been caught up in this Platonic view of a spiritual afterlife, others had reached a different conclusion. For example, according to Jewish historian Josephus (AD 37–100), the Sadducees held that "the soul perishes with the body". This view, of course, fuelled their debates with Jesus on the possibility of resurrection.

So Jesus was born into a world awash with diverse views about the afterlife and the age to come. Was it a purely spiritual world, as those influenced by Plato maintained, or was there in fact no afterlife, as the Sadducees taught?

Jesus was Jewish

Many Jews had not in fact wavered from the Old Testament hope that God would restore a Jewish community, secure within its own borders and free from the political domination of the Roman over-lords and it is most likely that Jesus would have grown up with the mainline Jewish belief (which we have just explored) that the age to come would be an existence firmly rooted on the earth. Jerusalem would be restored as a centre of worship, the land would be restored to the Jewish nation and all life would be touched by amazing fruitfulness and beauty. Social justice would be done; the poor would be cared for and other hopeless people (widows, orphans, foreigners) provided for and treated with respect.

The idea that the earth is destined for destruction in order to be replaced by 'heaven' would not have been on Jesus' school curriculum! 'Within mainline Jewish writings . . . there is virtu-ally no evidence that Jews were expecting the end of the space-time universe. They believed that the present world order would come to an end – the world in which pagans held power, and Jews, the covenant people of the Creator God, did not. Jews simply did not believe that the space-time order was shortly to disappear' (Tom Wright).[2]

Jesus almost certainly grew up with this framework of belief about 'the age to come' but did he reject it? Was it he who replaced this 'restored earth' view with a 'spiritual heaven'? Let us look at some of his teaching about the future.

Jesus promised to return to earth

In several passages Jesus teaches, explicitly or implicitly, that the end of this present era will be brought about by his return *to the earth*.[3]

Luke records Jesus' own words about the climax of the end-times: 'People will faint from fear and foreboding of what is coming upon the world, for the powers of the heavens will be shaken. Then they will see "the Son of Man coming in a cloud" with power and great glory'.[4]

Later, after his death and resurrection, the apostles, perturbed at Jesus' departure to heaven (in C S Lewis' words, through a 'fold in space'), were comforted with the promise that he would 'come in the same way as [they] saw him go into heaven'.[5] Come where? 'Back to earth' is the only possible answer.

Jesus further revealed this wonderful expectation in several parables that are commonly taken to have end-time significance, for example, the master coming home to judge the faithfulness of his servants,[6] or the bridegroom who arrives at the wedding feast to be greeted by the bridesmaids who had been there waiting for him.[7] Notice that Jesus is pictured as returning to where his servants are waiting and as arriving at the wedding; servants and wedding guests are not whisked off to be with him!

The end of this age then, according to Jesus, would be marked by *his* return to earth not *our* removal to heaven. Perhaps the only passage which appears at first reading to contradict this claim is that recorded in John 14, where Jesus tells his disciples that he is about to go to his 'Father's house' to prepare places for them and that one day he would return to take them to himself, so that where he is they may be also. Does this not imply that the disciples would go to Jesus (and the Father) and not vice versa?

As is their custom, commentators disagree over the meaning of this promise that Jesus made to his disciples, but one possible way of summarizing their understanding of it may be through the following paraphrase:

'In my Father's presence [ie house] there is room for all. As I go to the Father via the cross I prepare the means for you to enter his presence wherever you may find yourselves. Having opened the way for you to enjoy the same intimacy with the Father that you have seen me enjoy, I will return to you in the form of the Spirit, so that even whilst you live on earth you will share with me in the heavenly places.'

This concurs well with Jesus' statement later in the same chapter that 'those who love me will keep my word, and my Father will love them, and we will come to them and make our home with them'. Jesus is not trying to teach his disciples about his second coming, but rather trying to comfort them by explaining that his imminent departure is for their good as it will open the way to even greater intimacy with God (Father, Son and Spirit) than they had enjoyed during his earthly relationship with them.

If this passage is not concerned with the second coming, it cannot contradict the passages already referred to in which Jesus foresees his end-of-the-age return to earth as the trigger for the renewal of an earthly kingdom.

Jesus promised to renew all things

Matthew wrote about the effect of Jesus' return as being 'the renewal of all things'.[8] Contrary to popular expectation, then, Jesus is coming back to the earth to renew creation not to destroy it. Only when Jesus returns will all that exists in God's creation be liberated from the brokenness foisted on it by Adam's rebellion and subsequent human sinfulness.

On Jesus' return, the words of God in Revelation will thunder through the earth: 'See, I am making all things new'.[9] What a day! For the first time ever we shall see the earth as God intended it to be – in all its breathtaking beauty – as the warping effects of sin are undone and creation is revealed in new glory.

Strange that whilst Jesus promised to return to the earth to renew it, so many of us, his followers, have been taught that we will have to escape to heaven because the earth is going to be destroyed!

Jesus promised to reward the faithful

On his return to earth, and as part of the consequent renewal, men and women who in this age have lived sacrificially for God will be rewarded for the price that they paid to follow him. Those who gave up family or possessions for the sake of Jesus will be fully repaid.[10] It will be as though every sacrifice had been an investment in heaven's bank, and at Jesus' return the vaults will be opened and each person repaid with interest! This is surely what Jesus meant when he taught his disciples not to store up treasures on earth but to store up treasures in heaven.[11] Heaven's bank will pay its customers on the earth in the age to come. The idea that you actually have to go to heaven to enjoy your reward is like imagining that you have to spend your life savings in the bank where your account is held![12]

Jesus frequently pictured humanity as divided into two groups, 'the wheat and the weeds', 'the good and the bad fish', 'the wheat and the chaff' or 'the sheep and goats'.[13] The wheat, the good fish and the sheep are symbols of those who will be rewarded for their faith in God (as demonstrated in the way that they have lived) and the weeds, the bad fish and the goats symbolize those who will be condemned by their lack of faith.

One of the most extended passages dealing with this aspect of final judgment is the parable of the sheep and goats in Matthew 25:31–46. Jesus, having returned to earth (v31), divides humanity into 'sheep' (the faithful) and 'goats' (the faithless). The sheep, as reward for their faithfulness in living out their love for God by serving their fellow man, are invited to 'come' to Jesus and inherit the fullness of the reign of God. The goats, however, as punishment for their faith*less*ness – evidenced in their self-centred living – are told to 'depart . . . into the eternal fire prepared for the devil and his angels' (v41) and to 'go away into eternal punishment' (v46).

It is, of course, unwise to attempt to squeeze too much doctrinal detail out of a parable, and I confess that I skate on thin theological ice in these next two paragraphs, but it is interesting to ponder on what is happening here. The faithful sheep gather to the Shepherd (standing on the earth), whilst the faithless goats are sent away into a place of punishment. This is surely a reversal of a commonly held view on judgement in which it is the faithful who have to *go away* (to heaven) whilst the wicked are left behind to be burned up along with the earth.

Luke affirmed that it will be the wicked not the righteous who must leave the earth, by drawing a parallel between the days of Noah and the return of Jesus.[14] Just as the flood destroyed the wicked from the face of the earth, so Jesus will return and do likewise. Luke warned that judgement will come at an hour when it is not expected and that as people go about their ordinary business 'one will be taken and the other left'. This passage has often been used to terrify people about being left behind on the earth whilst the righteous are swept up to heaven. But in Noah's day it was Noah and his family who were left to live on the earth and the wicked who were swept away by the flood-tide of God's anger! Somehow the roles have been reversed!

Maybe we should pray that we are not those who are forced to depart the earth (as the goats were) into hellish punishment but those who are left behind to enjoy the rewards of the faithful on the renewed earth with Jesus.

Jesus reveals a big picture
So, did Jesus continue to uphold Jewish teaching that God's future purpose was to restore Israel to her land? Well, yes and no! Certainly Jesus' end-time teaching can be understood as being physical and earthly rather than spiritual and heavenly. Only if you read his words with preconceived notions of what you expect him to say does he actually say it! However, in one important way he does *develop* the Jewish belief of a renewed homeland.

In Matthew 5:5 Jesus quotes from Psalm 37:11. The psalm says that 'the meek shall inherit the land, and delight themselves in abundant prosperity'. Inheriting the land, as we have seen, was indeed what the Jews were hoping for, but Jesus broadens the canvas considerably: 'Blessed are the meek, for they will inherit the earth'. Now it must be said that Jesus could simply have been re-stating the Old Testament promise with different language, but it would appear that he is deliberately broadening the promise to embrace the whole earth as the inheritance of the saints. Certainly this is the view of (amongst others) theologian G C Berkouwer who writes, 'In Jesus' promise this passage assumes eschatological import: the land that the meek shall possess is no longer Canaan, but the new earth . . .'[15] Whereas the faithful meek of Israel looked forward to a restored promised land, the meek believer in Jesus anticipates a restored earth.

The destiny of the meek, like the destiny of the first man and woman, is to inherit the wonderful earth that God has created. With the return of Jesus, the Old Testament prophecies of future blessing on earth will come true, not just for the Jews in Israel but for all God's faithful people of all ages in the whole world. As Habakkuk put it, 'the earth will be filled with the knowledge of the glory of the Lord, as the waters cover the sea'![16]

What a wonderful hope, but sadly 'this cosmic aspect of redemption was increasingly lost to Western Christendom since the Age of Enlightenment, and to this day we have been unable to restore it to its strength and clarity' (A Koberle).[17] However, Jesus *was* clear about this 'aspect of redemption', so let us look at the rest of the New Testament to see if what we find there gives us any cause to abandon the future hope of renewed creation.

PAUL'S VIEW

Life in the overlap

One of the great themes of Paul's writings is the tension between the 'new' blessings – ie what Jesus has secured for believers in the present age – and the 'not yet' blessings – ie what will only be enjoyed in the age to come. Whilst Paul clearly teaches that the benefits of Jesus' death, resurrection and ascension are to be experienced now, he also speaks of an inheritance for the future, of which present blessings are only a down payment. Commenting on this now-but-not-yet present age he says, 'For now we see in a mirror, dimly, but then we will see face to face. Now I know only in part; then I will know fully . . .'[18] Salvation for Paul is past tense, 'I have been saved';[19] present tense, 'I am being saved';[20] and future tense, 'I shall be saved'.[21] There is a very real sense that in this present age we have enough of God's blessings to satisfy our hunger for spiritual reality but not enough to fill us. We have the first-fruits of blessing to nibble at, but the full-blown banquet has not yet begun.

Free at last
Fascinatingly, Paul applies this teaching not just to human experience but also to the whole created order. The world itself is existing in an era of frustrating incompleteness. Having been damaged by centuries of sinful abuse and neglect, it also longs for its salvation and restoration.

> For the creation waits with eager longing for the revealing of the children of God; for the creation was subjected to futility, not of its own will but by the will of the one who subjected it, in hope that the creation itself will be set free from its bondage to decay and will obtain the freedom of the glory of the children of God. We know that the whole creation has been groaning in labour pains until now . . .[22]

Note that the creation is waiting for freedom and glory not for destruction; for Paul, the earth itself has a future hope.

Paul further reveals that this glorious salvation of creation is made possible by the work of Jesus on the cross. On the cross, Jesus, in whom 'all things in heaven and on earth were created', took on himself the brokenness of his own creation. Raised to resurrection life, he now has 'first place in everything' and it is his very presence in heaven which assures that 'all things hold together'. The created order, thus sustained by its mighty redeeming Creator, can now look forward to its own healing and reconciliation with its Maker, because through Jesus 'God was pleased to reconcile to himself all things, whether on earth or in heaven, by making peace through the blood of his cross.'[23]

All too often we think of Jesus' redeeming work as applying only to repentant sinners, but he died to eradicate the presence and the power of sin from *all* things. Because Jesus died, his world can be saved from sin just as surely as can you and I.

Heirs to a new world

For Paul, the fact that Jesus is Lord and that Jesus has saved us gives us hope and the assurance of an inheritance for the future.[24] But what is this inheritance? According to Tom Wright in his commentary on Colossians, the language of 'inheritance' 'evokes a whole world of imagery relating to Israel's exodus from Egypt and her entry into the promised land'. The difference now is that Israel's inheritance of Canaan is 'widened into the promise of a whole new creation' for God's New Testament people.[25]

Paul and Jesus both appear to anticipate that the age to come will be an age of *earthly* bliss. Creation itself will be restored and mankind will be enabled finally to enjoy it in the way that God first intended.

Certainly the age to come will see this world 'flavoured' with God's presence in a way which, this side of the return of Jesus, we can only begin to imagine. Nevertheless, the fact that it will be *this world* does allow us to view the future with a degree of certainty. 'If the future is an unknown "reality", why do the Old and the New Testaments not talk about an unknown "x" – an unknown quantity – instead of arousing these various concepts of what the new heaven and the new earth will be like and talking about the longing of *creation* for freedom from its perishability?' (G C Berkouwer).[26]

Bodies of evidence

A final piece of evidence from Paul's theology which supports a future earthly hope is to be found in his staunch defence of physical resurrection. We shall return to this theme in chapter five; for now we will simply note that Paul strongly refutes any notion of a spiritual afterlife akin to modern conceptions of heaven, and insists that we are all promised physical resurrection. In so doing he suggests that the spiritual state of existence which we enter at death is not our final one. The belief that we go to heaven when we die is very true,[27] but to imagine that we then stay in heaven for all eternity is much harder to support biblically! We are ultimately bound for new bodies in which to enjoy life on the new earth – I believe that is the only way to make sense of the promise of physical resurrection, a view endorsed by G C Berkouwer: 'the resurrection body is not an abstract, spiritual existence having nothing to do with the earth, but something that has a place and a manifold function *in* the earth'.[28]

PETER'S VIEW

Bonfire night
It is in Peter's second letter that we get closest to the scenario of this earth being destroyed in judgement.

> But the day of the Lord will come like a thief, and then the heavens will pass away with a loud noise, and the elements will be dissolved with fire, and the earth and everything that is done on it will be disclosed.
> Since all these things are to be dissolved in this way, what sort of persons ought you to be in leading lives of holiness and godliness, waiting for and hastening the coming of the day of God, because of which the heavens will be set ablaze and dissolved, and the elements will melt with fire?[29]

Before looking at this in a bit more detail, it is worth noting that 'the idea that the world will finally be annihilated by fire appears only in 2 Peter in the New Testament, and is indeed in its fully developed form not biblical at all' (John N D Kelly).[30] Doubtless the idea of an end-time conflagration has been promoted by the language of the Authorised Version of the Bible which translates verse 10b as 'the earth also and the works that are therein shall be burned up'.

The fire that purifies

Actually the case is far from proven by these verses. Fire in the Bible is frequently linked with the idea of purifying something that is corrupt. In the act of purification the fire does two things: it destroys the impurities, and thus reveals that which is pure. The biblical fire of end-time judgement is frequently pictured as having this same double function, both destroying God's enemies and refining or 'testing' his people.

Psalm 97:3 says, 'Fire goes before him [the Lord], and consumes his adversaries on every side', a theme that is awesomely reiterated in the New Testament: 'For if we wilfully persist in sin after having received the knowledge of the truth, there no longer remains a sacrifice for sins, but a fearful prospect of judgement, and a fury of fire that will consume the adversaries'.[31] Paul, however, wrote of a judgemental fire which will 'test what sort of work each has done' by destroying anything that is unworthy, thus revealing what survives the fire to be of eternal merit.[32]

Holding that thought in mind, let us return to the judgement which God wrought on the earth in Noah's day. Peter puts his statement about end-time fire in the context of the Flood story.[33] We noted in chapter one that before judging the earth with water God had said that he would destroy the earth.[34] However, what he actually did was to destroy all *wickedness* from the face of the earth, washing the earth clean for humanity to live on. Henry Alford comments, 'The flood did not annihilate the earth, but changed it; and as the new earth was the consequence of the flood, so the final heavens and earth shall be of the fire.'[35]

So it is interesting that Peter himself paralleled his end-time judgement of fire to Noah's flood. Like the flood, the fire will destroy the godless[36] and disclose the earth[37] in its sin-free form for the first time since the days of the Fall. Peter's powerful imagery of judgemental fire may thus be seen as portraying a fire that purifies by destroying all godlessness, rather than a fire that destroys everything.

Fire walking

Although it is not its major purpose in scripture, the Old Testament story of Shadrach, Meshach and Abednego[38] may be seen as an interesting illustration of the end-time fire of judgement (although, like all illustrations, it should not be pressed too far!).

King Nebuchadnezzar prepared a super-heated fire to punish Shadrach, Meshach and Abednego for refusing to worship his statue. The fire of punishment was so hot that Nebuchadnezzar's servants who threw the three men into the furnace were themselves destroyed. However, the very same fire that destroyed the servants of the wicked king left the servants of God unharmed. Far from being destroyed, they were marked out or revealed as God's men and vindicated before Nebuchadnezzar and all who looked on.

Maybe the end-time fire of judgement will be a similar fire; a fire of God's wrath that consumes all wickedness but through which believers, and the earth itself, will be preserved unharmed. When we walk through the fire, we shall not be burned and the flame shall not consume us because God has redeemed us.[39]

This view of a fire that both destroys and purifies finds further support in Peter's vision of 'new heavens and a new earth, where righteousness is at home'.[40] Peter is re-stating in a New Testament age the Old Testament prophesy of Isaiah[41] in which God declared, 'I am about to create new heavens and a new earth'.

It is important to note that the creation of the new earth will be different from the creation of the earth on which we now live in one vital respect. The clue to that difference lies in the use of the Greek words *kainos* and *neos*. Both are translated in English as 'new'; *kainos* denotes 'that which is better than the old, whereas *neos* is used for that which has not yet been, that which has just made its appearance'.[42]

When God first made the earth, it was *neos*. It had never existed; it was not a new model based on an old pattern; God created it out of nothing ('ex nihilo' as the theologians say!).

However, according to Peter and to John,[43] our future is to be spent on a *kainos* earth – an earth that is a new improved version of the one that has already existed.

JOHN'S VIEW

In our voyage towards understanding the future of the New Testament we must finally sail, albeit briefly, the stormy waters of John's great vision – the book of Revelation.

Revelation is often presented as the Bible's telescope trained on the future. By looking through it carefully, we are told, we can gain God's perspective on future events. If only we can interpret the rich symbolism that it contains, then we shall be able to chart the progress of human history from here to eternity (to coin a phrase!).

Revelation, however, is much more than a divinely disguised map outlining the future. At the start of the book Jesus tells John to 'write what you have seen, what is, and what is to take place after this'.[44] The book then has two functions: in its deeply symbolic scenes we are being shown both something that *is* and something that *will be*.

But what is this revelation of? What exactly is being revealed? Apocalyptic writing such as that found in Revelation, which is typified by colourful and bizarre imagery, should be seen not so much as a peep into the future as a peep behind the curtains of the present, revealing the spiritual events in the heavenly places that are shaping life on earth. Strangely, an example from a non-apocalyptic passage in the Old Testament will serve to give us an insight into what is going on in true apocalyptic writing in the Bible.

In 2 Kings 6:15–17, the Syrian army have crept up at night and surrounded the home of Elisha in order to arrest him. Whilst Elisha slept, his servant got up, went outside and came face to face with Syrians – lots of them! He rushed back to Elisha, full of anxiety and despair.

'Alas, master, what shall we do?' he enquired.

Elisha, being more aware of the proximity and reality of

God's heavenly army than his servant, answered, 'Don't be afraid, for there are more with us than there are with them.'

The servant must have wondered what his master was going on about! He knew, or at least he *thought* he knew, that there were just the two of them.

But Elisha was praying even as his servant was wondering:

'O Lord, please open his eyes that he may see.'
So the Lord opened the eyes of the servant, and he saw . . .

What did he see? He saw the armies of heaven: 'the mountain was full of horses and chariots of fire all around Elisha'. For a brief instant Elisha's servant was privileged to see heaven opened, and the sight put his human situation into heaven's perspective. No longer alone. No longer needing to fear. God was present with his army and no Aramean task force was going to outsmart that lot![45]

This revelation of what is happening in the 'heavenly places' is, in large measure, what is going on in the book of Revelation. We are permitted, with John, to enter through heaven's open door[46] and Jesus himself gives us a guided tour! We can affirm, then, that 'as a literary genre, "apocalyptic" is a way of investing space-time events with their theological significance' (Tom Wright),[47] not merely a way of predicting the future.

Jesus gave this tremendous vision to us to permit us to see behind the scenes of Christian struggle in every age into the heavenly battles that are shaping world events. Richard Bewes has written, 'You can get too clever with the book of Revelation. The vision was intended to comfort and prepare us, not to test our ingenuity'.[48]

To Christian individuals and churches the message of Revelation is 'God wins'! We look into the spiritual conflict underlying human destiny and see that evil is ultimately destroyed, that it is the *Lamb* who is unrolling the scroll of history, that it is *God* who is on the throne, that it is the *Messiah* who will reign for ever and ever, that it is the *Son of Man* who will wield the sickle of end-time harvesting, and that it is the *Word of God* who is the victorious King of kings.[49] By allowing us to look into heaven we are given hope for life on earth. The vision does indeed 'comfort' us as it reveals what is happening in the heavenly places *now*.

Revelation also reveals something of what is to take place at the end of this age. There are hints of a glorious climax throughout the book, but in chapters 21 and 22 the statements are bold and plain. After watching the destruction of Satan, death and all evil,[50] John writes:

> Then I saw a new heaven and a new earth; for the first heaven and the first earth had passed away . . . And I saw the holy city, the new Jerusalem, coming down out of heaven from God . . . And I heard a loud voice from the throne saying,
>
> > 'See, the home of God is among mortals.
> > He will dwell with them as their God;
> > they will be his peoples,
> > and God himself will be with them;
> > he will wipe every tear from their eyes.
> > Death will be no more;
> > mourning and crying and pain will be no more,
> > For the first things have passed away.'
>
> And the one who was seated on the throne said, 'See, I am making all things new.'[51]

Apocalyptic language (like parables and illustrations) must not be pressed too literally, but what wonderful, awe-inspiring, hope-inducing words. Can you begin to envisage it? The whole world healed. Creation delivered from its 'bondage to decay' and humanity set free. But most amazing of all, God is going to 'dwell' with us. Did you notice that it is not the inhabitants of earth who will go to heaven but the Inhabitant of the heavenly places who will come to earth? The new Jerusalem comes down out of heaven and God, as it were, moves house. He takes up residence at the centre of the creation he loves so much so that his dwelling is now with humankind. What an amazing reunion of Creator and created! Once again he will walk with us in the garden of earth,[52] and as his loving presence soaks into every part and person on the globe so the effects of the Fall will be finally banished. 'The kingdom of the world' will finally become 'the kingdom of our Lord and of his Messiah, and he will reign for ever and ever'.[53]

At long last those Old Testament promises to Israel, broadened to include the church's inheritance of the whole earth, will have come to pass. God's home, that is heaven, will have come to earth and all things shall be made new.

NOTES ON CHAPTER 2

1 C McDannell & B Lang *'Heaven – A History'* (Yale University Press, 1990, p16ff) had made an impact on people's expectations of the age to come, making it more 'spiritual' and less 'physical'.

2 N T Wright, *The New Testament and the people of God*, Society for Promoting Christian Knowledge (SPCK), 1992, p392.

3 Eg Matthew 24:30; 25:31.

4 Luke 21:26,27.

5 Acts 1:11.

6 Matthew 25:14–19.

7 Matthew 25:1–13.

8 Matthew 19:28.

9 Revelation 21:5.

10 Mark 10:29–30.

11 Matthew 6:19–20.

12 See chapters three and seven for more on 'rewards'.

13 Matthew 13:24–30; 13:47–50; 3:12; 25:31–46.

14 Luke 17:24–37.

15 G C Berkouwer, *The return of Christ*, Wm B Eerdmans Publishing Co (US), p213.

16 Habakkuk 2:14.

17 A Koberle, from *Der Herr Über Alles*, quoted in *The return of Christ*, see above, p103.
18 1 Corinthians 13:12.
19 Ephesians 2:8.
20 1 Corinthians 1:18.
21 Romans 13:11.
22 Romans 8:19–22.
23 Colossians 1:15–20.
24 Colossians 1:12.
25 N T Wright, *Colossians*, Tyndale New Testament Commentaries, Inter-Varsity Press, 1987, p61.
26 *The return of Christ*, see above, p232.
27 See chapters three and four.
28 *The return of Christ*, see above.
29 2 Peter 3:10–12.
30 John N D Kelly, *The epistles of Peter and of Jude*, New Testament Commentaries, A & C Black, 1969, p360.
31 Hebrews 10:26–27.
32 1 Corinthians 3:13.
33 2 Peter 3:5–6.
34 Genesis 6:13.
35 Henry Alford, *The Greek New Testament: an exegetical and critical commentary*, vol 4, part 2, p418.
36 2 Peter 3:7.
37 2 Peter 3:10.
38 Daniel 3.
39 Isaiah 43:1–5.
40 2 Peter 3:13.
41 Isaiah 65:17.
42 Colin Brown (ed), *The New International Dictionary of New Testament theology*, vol 2, Paternoster Press, 1976, p670.
43 Revelation 21:1.
44 Revelation 1:19.
45 I am grateful to Tom Wright for this Old Testament illustration of the true nature of apocalyptic writing.
46 Revelation 4:1.

47   *The New Testament and the people of God*, see above, p392.

48   Richard Bewes, *The church overcomes*, Mowbray (Cassell), 1984, p87.

49   Revelation 20:10; 5:6–9; 7:10; 11:15; 14:14–16; 19:13,16.

50   Revelation 20:7–10.

51   Revelation 21:1,3–5.

52   Genesis 3:8.

53   Revelation 11:15.

Chapter 3

SO WHAT ABOUT HEAVEN?

All this talk of an eternally *earthly* future may have left some readers feeling confused. If the inheritance of the righteous meek is the earth (as Jesus claimed) then what *is* heaven? When the Bible uses the word 'heaven', or 'the heavens', it is sometimes merely talking about the sky or the physical 'world above our heads' (eg God's injunction to Abraham in Genesis 15:5 to 'look toward heaven and count the stars'). However, as the Bible story unfolds so does our understanding of 'heaven', and it is this we shall now explore.

HEAVEN – INVISIBLE REALITY

The first thing we should note is that heaven is real! It is no less real than the world we can see. In a materialist, rationalist age it is sometimes hard to hang on to belief in the invisible reality of heaven. In Western culture we are brought up with the idea that 'what you see is what there is' and concepts of an invisible spirit world surrounding ours are frowned upon. However, if we allow the Bible to inform our view of reality we are forced, in the words of Francis Schaeffer, to believe that 'there is an unseen portion [of the world] as well as a seen portion . . . They are not mutually exclusive, but are parts of one reality . . . To understand reality in our universe properly, you have to consider both halves – both the seen and the unseen'.[1]

It is impossible to read the Bible and not realize that its message is incomprehensible from a purely materialistic world view. God himself is spirit[2] and he is surrounded by spirits (angels).[3] It is this invisible world of spiritual existence that the Bible calls heaven.

HEAVEN – GOD'S HOME

The most helpful way of understanding the meaning of 'heaven' when it appears in the Bible is as 'the dimension in which God exists'. Ecclesiastes 5:2 puts it plainly: 'God is in heaven, and you upon earth'. Other scriptures also underline this distinction between God's natural home and ours: 'The heavens are the Lord's heavens, but the earth he has given to human beings'.[4]

One of the remarkable things about Jesus' relationship with his Father was the sense of closeness and intimacy that they shared. Jesus clearly did not see the Father as dwelling in a different land somewhere out beyond the moon. Although he prayed to his Father *in heaven*, his prayers were spoken as though his Father were actually next to him.[5] Heaven was not a place 'out there' but an invisible dimension. 'The idea of location is not important, for it is never enlarged upon in the words of Jesus. Heaven is where God is . . . We may conclude therefore that for Jesus, heaven stood for the dwelling place of God' (Donald Guthrie).[6]

But what about the frequent references throughout the Bible to looking 'up' to heaven? Jesus 'looked up to heaven' before blessing the five loaves and two fish that were to feed the 5,000 men;[7] Luke records that Jesus was 'taken up to heaven';[8] and Paul looks forward to a day when 'the Lord himself will come down from heaven'.[9]

Surely these references, and others like them, lead us to believe that heaven is a place 'out there' or, more precisely, 'up there'? Not necessarily. It could be that this idea of heaven being 'up' is merely a way of stating its 'otherness'. Heaven is different to 'down' and 'around'; it is invisible and, most supremely, it is where God dwells in all his glory. The idea of 'up' reinforces the holiness and majesty of God and the awe-full difference between heaven and earth whilst not necessarily saying anything about heavenly geography. 'Looking *up* to heaven is a reminder that God is not earthbound', rather than saying anything about the location of a place (Donald Guthrie).[10]

With this perspective of heaven as the all-present home of the Father, it is possible to understand Jesus' mission to earth not as a cosmic journey from heaven 'up there' but as a stepping across from the heavenly realm of infinite, yet invisible, existence into a finite, visible earthly body. He is the true bread from heaven;[11] indeed he is the only one to have so completely bridged the gulf between the invisible and the visible aspects of creation: 'No one has ascended into heaven except the one who descended from heaven, the Son of Man'.[12]

HEAVEN – A WORLD AT WAR

Whilst it is true that heaven is presented in the Bible as 'the dwelling place of God', this is not the whole picture. God is presented as King of the spirits; the supreme Creator and Ruler of heaven and earth,[13] owner of the heavens,[14] and the one seated on heaven's throne.[15] Yet in this exalted position he is not pictured as dwelling in splendid isolation. Heaven buzzes with activity; it is filled with other equally real, yet invisible, creatures called angels.

Angels are God's messengers and servants, created to work for him in the business of running the cosmos. They are sometimes sent on brief operations into the material world to communicate God's heart to human beings,[16] but their main responsibilities lie in heaven and may be summarized under three headings – they are worshippers, wardens and warriors.

The *worship* that angels offer to God is often referred to in the Bible. Worshipping angels feature prominently in the glimpse into heaven given to John in his Revelation.

> Then I looked, and I heard the voice of many angels surrounding the throne and the living creatures and the elders; they numbered myriads of myriads and thousands of thousands, singing with full voice,

'Worthy is the Lamb that was slaughtered
to receive power and wealth and wisdom and might
and honour and glory and blessing!'[17]

It is not surprising that creatures who are privileged to share God's home should be so struck by his presence that praise and worship become a natural and central part of existence.

Angels as *wardens* may seem a less familiar concept. A warden is someone who 'has the charge or care of something, especially one who is responsible for the enforcement of certain regulations'.[18] It is in this sense that angels are identified in the book of Revelation as working under Jesus as wardens of history. As God's plan unfolds it is angels who blow the trumpets, carry the scrolls, wield the sickles, pour out the bowls and bind Satan in the pit.[19] Without going into what this symbolic activity means, it is noticeable that angels are used by God and act under his authority to be wardens of the heavenly acts which shape human destiny. The work they are directed to do in the heavenly places affects the unfolding drama of human history on the earth.

Third, angels are *warriors*. Revelation 12:7 observes that 'war broke out in heaven' between two spiritual powers (Michael and 'the dragon'). Satan (himself an angel, remember) attracted a large number of angelic beings to follow him; ever since they have been warring against God's purposes in heaven and on earth.

God created all angels, but not all are now loyal to him. Daniel is given privileged insight into this struggle when, in response to his prayer and fasting, an angel appears to him and tells him of the spiritual warfare that he (the angel) has had to fight in order to answer Daniel's prayers.[20]

Paul says that the rogue angels under Satan's usurped authority are our real enemy since (he implies) their heavenly activity harms life on earth just as the activity of the warden angels enhances it. This is what Paul advises:

Put on the whole armour of God, so that you may be able to stand against the wiles of the devil. For our struggle is not against enemies of blood and flesh, but against the rulers, against the authorities, against the cosmic powers of this present darkness, against the spiritual forces of evil in the heavenly places.[21]

HEAVEN – WORLD OF THE DEAD

We have moved from a view of heaven as our 'future home' to one of 'an invisible world of reality', so far inhabited by God and two categories of angel – those loyal to him and those in rebellion against him. Is that the full complement of heaven's population? Not quite.

Heaven is the world in which all spiritual beings have their current existence. God, angels *and* the spirits of human beings who have died. We shall return to this 'realm' of heaven in some detail in chapter four but, for the sake of completeness in this analysis of heaven's population, we must note here that when a human's body dies, a part of them, their spirit (or soul, if you like), lives on. But where does it live? In the world of invisible reality called heaven.

We have already observed that the book of Revelation gives us our clearest insight into the spirit world that the Bible calls heaven. As the Holy Spirit inspires and informs John's vision, he sees 'those who had been slaughtered for the word of God and for the testimony they had given'[22] – the spirits of people who had been martyred for their faith already consciously enjoying and participating in the life and worship of heaven.

This vision is consistent with the biblical view of dead human beings entering a new spiritual existence in 'the world of the dead'[23] and underpins the comfort given to those who grieve that their lost Christian relatives or friends have indeed 'gone to heaven to be with Jesus'. Death marks the point of transition from the physical world of life on earth to the spiritual world of life in heaven.

Heaven's population is now comprised of three categories of spiritual being:

1   God: heaven's Creator and King.
2   Angels: God's heavenly work force, some of whom are in rebellion.
3   Dead humanity: alive in spirit form, awaiting final judgement.

HEAVEN – IMPACTING LIFE ON EARTH

'It is essential to note that Jesus never envisaged a [purely] "future" heaven which bore no relation to present experience' (Donald Guthrie).[24] Traditional views of heaven as an 'up there', almost exclusively future reality fail to be true to the Bible's message that heaven interacts with earth *now* and that the world of God and his angels is close at hand.

> A proper Christian understanding of heaven is not as a place remote from the present world, but rather as a dimension, normally kept secret, of present reality . . . 'Heaven' is God's dimension of present reality (Tom Wright).[25]

Heaven is present tense, close at hand and able to affect daily life in what we like to call 'the real world'. Paul's teaching is that Christians enjoy a privileged status in heaven – already. We have been blessed in Christ Jesus with 'every spiritual blessing in the heavenly places'.[26] The presence of God's Holy Spirit in the life of a believer bridges the gap between the invisible world of heaven and the physical world of humanity, making the powerful 'heavenly' presence of God a very real 'earthly' experience. A rich truth celebrated in Graham Kendrick's joyful song, 'Oh, heaven is in my heart'. It's true! The spirit of the King of heaven has entered my earthly existence. Amazing!

Paul expresses the same truth in a slightly different way when he declares that 'our citizenship is in heaven'.[27] This does not mean that we have to live in heaven or that one day we will be going there. The challenge is to recognize that our humanity, our values and our view of the world need to be shaped by God from heaven. God calls us to live in the culture of a fallen earth without conforming to its norms, being intent instead on transforming earth by living out the values of heaven. We are the light of the world[28] and that light shines from heaven onto earth through us.

Trying to live as Christians in our own strength would be impossible because all our activities, from prayer and worship to social action and evangelism, depend on the spiritual resources of God enhancing and directing our human efforts. For example, it is only because 'all authority in *heaven* and on earth has been given to' Jesus[29] that we can go about the business of making disciples for him with any hope of success. Drawing on the resources of Jesus' ultimate heavenly authority, we can see people on earth set free from the kingdom of Satan's bogus heavenly power. Fruitful evangelism thus illustrates that heavenly authority empowers earthly activity.

Jesus asserted that the heart of our hopes and prayers in this age is to see God's rule – his kingdom – affect life on earth in such a way that his will is done on earth even as it is being done in heaven.[30] God's rule in heaven defines and shapes his rule on earth. The invisible shapes the visible, the supernatural moulds the natural, and the spiritual influences the material. Heaven and earth are linked in a present-tense relationship, and Christians need to learn to think more about heaven's authority in their lives than about its accessibility at their death.

HEAVEN – GOD'S STORE-CUPBOARD

Jesus made considerable demands on those who would be his followers; in fact at times he was quite willing to watch people turn away from him rather than attract a crowd of half-hearted followers-at-any-price. The demands of discipleship were presented in terms of sacrifice and cost; priority had to be given – at the expense of family, career and personal security – to the kingdom of God.[31] (We might compare this somewhat blunt evangelistic approach with the no-strings-attached God-loves-you-anyway style of gospel that we are at times tempted to offer in our desire to see people accept Jesus!)

However, often in the same breath as demanding complete self-sacrifice from his followers he assures them that their sacrifices are being recorded by God and in some way being put 'on deposit' in heaven, to be repaid with interest in the future.

> 'Blessed are you when people revile you and persecute you and utter all kinds of evil against you falsely on my account. Rejoice and be glad, for your reward is great in heaven . . . [32]

> 'Do not store up for yourselves treasures on the earth, where moth and rust consume and where thieves break in and steal; but store up for yourselves treasures in heaven . . .'[33]

> 'Sell all that you own and distribute the money to the poor, and you will have treasure in heaven; then come, follow me.'[34]

William Lane comments, 'The frank recognition of the loss that allegiance to Jesus and the gospel may entail is conditioned by the fact that all that is lost in one society will be regained a hundredfold in the new society created by the dynamic of the gospel.'[35]

These promises of rewards kept in heaven for the faithful clearly became of great importance to the New Testament church when persecution struck. Peter, having heard the promises first-hand from Jesus, encouraged the struggling churches of Asia Minor by reminding them of their 'inheritance that is imperishable, undefiled, and unfading, kept in heaven' for them.[36]

It is a wonderful thought, that every act of service which we render and every loss which we suffer in our attempts to make Jesus known are logged in God's 'computer' for the great payout on Judgement Day. Those who have made great sacrifices will get a great inheritance from heaven's bank, whilst those who have lived selfishly will find an overdraft awaiting them. It is in this sense that Christians who are last in this age's scheme of things, poor people, perhaps of low reputation and status, will be first in the kingdom. The widow who gave her last farthing for the Lord's work will find a great bonus on deposit, whilst the rich young ruler who insisted on hanging onto what he had will be served with a bill for account charges that he just cannot meet.[37] The prospect of seeing the humble poor exalted above the proud and rich on that great day will surely bring tears of joy to anyone who truly hungers and thirsts after righteousness.

HEAVEN – TO BE CLEANSED

As we confidently look forward to a new earth as our eternal home, we should not lose sight of the promise that heaven too will be judged and cleansed. If God were merely to renew the earth and to place on it a redeemed humanity, we would be back to the situation in Eden. Great, you might think, but wait a minute: Eden, as well as being the scene of creative perfection, was the scene of humanity's fall from relationship with God. How do we know that when God places redeemed humanity on the renewed earth in the age to come the whole sorry cycle will not repeat itself? This is a very vexed question, but clues to an answer may be found by understanding that, in the age to come, not only the earth but also the heavens will be renewed.

In Eden the world was 'very good' and Adam and Eve were sinless; but heaven was already 'polluted' and Satan was able to twist God's good creation by tempting humanity to adopt his attitude of rebellion against God. The initial problem was not creation, not humanity, and certainly not God, but the presence of spiritual wickedness in the heavenly places. And here is the one huge difference between creation as we know it and renewed creation as we hope for it. The Bible says that not only will the earth be cleansed and renewed, but the heavens will also be judged and purified.

Isaiah, Peter and John all affirm that God will create 'new heavens and a new earth.'[38] The Day of the Lord will have cosmic implications; the unseen world of angels and departed human spirits will be judged (more on the latter in chapter four). Satan himself will be consigned to hell fire and, according to Jesus, all his angels will burn there with him.[39] The new heavens and new earth will be populated by loyal angels and redeemed humanity, united together in their love for God and their desire to serve him only for all eternity. There will be no accusing, condemning tempter moving through the new heavens 'looking for someone to devour' on the new earth.[40] Hallelujah again!

HEAVEN ON EARTH

Through the Holy Spirit we can begin to experience heaven on earth now. God's spiritual resources are made available to us by his Spirit living in us and acting through us to affect the shape of human life. It is marvellous. Gifts of healing, prophesying and the God-given power to work miracles are our inheritance in the here and now but, wonderful though that is, they are only shadows of the future reality. In the age to come the spiritual life of heaven will integrate with life on earth in such a way that the latter will be touched and beautified by God's presence.

Revelation 21:3–4, speaking of the new heavens and new earth that are to be created after final judgement and the destruction of evil, says, 'Now God's home is with human beings! He will live with them, and they shall be his people. God himself will be with them, and he will be their God' (Good News Bible).

'New, bodily human beings will need a new world in which to live. In this transformed world order, the veil will be lifted for all time. The realities of the heavenly world will be visibly united with the realities of earth' (Tom Wright).[41] No longer a sense of distance from an 'up there' heaven. No longer a struggle to 'break through' to God in prayer and praise. God's heavenly dwelling will be among his people. The life of heaven will suffuse life on earth, and all that exists on earth will be touched by its immanent presence.

What a prospect, to know the presence of the living God in all that we say, think, feel and do! Come quickly, Lord Jesus!

NOTES ON CHAPTER 3

1 Francis Schaeffer, *Death in the city*, Inter-Varsity Press, p112.
2 John 4:24.
3 Revelation 5:11.
4 Psalm 115:16.
5 Matthew 6:9.
6 Donald Guthrie, *New Testament theology*, Inter-Varsity Press, 1981, p875/6.
7 Matthew 14:19.
8 Acts 1:2.
9 1 Thessalonians 4:16 (NIV).
10 *New Testament theology*, see above.
11 John 6:31,32,41,45.
12 John 3:13.
13 Genesis 14:19.
14 Psalm 89:11.
15 Psalm 103:19.
16 Eg Genesis 16:7–12; Numbers 22:22–35; Luke 1:11–20; Acts 8:26.
17 Revelation 5:11–12.
18 The Collins Dictionary.
19 Revelation 8:6; 10:2; 14:17; 16:1; 20:1–3.
20 Daniel 10.
21 Ephesians 6:11,12.
22 Revelation 6:9.
23 See chapter four.
24 See chapter four.
25 N T Wright, Drew lecture, 1993, used with permission.
26 Ephesians 1:3.
27 Philippians 3:20.
28 Matthew 5:14.
29 Matthew 28:18.

30 Matthew 6:10.
31 Eg Matthew 10:37–39; Luke 14:25–33.
32 Matthew 5:11,12.
33 Matthew 6:19–20.
34 Luke 18:22.
35 William Lane, *The Gospel of Mark*, New International Commentaries on the New Testament, Eerdmans, 1974, p370; see also Mark 10:29–30.
36 1 Peter 1:3–4.
37 Luke 21:1–4; Mark 10:17–22.
38 Isaiah 65:17; 2 Peter 3:13; Revelation 21:1.
39 Revelation 20:10; Matthew 25:41.
40 *Cf* 1 Peter 5:8.
41 N T Wright, *The New Testament and the people of God*, SPCK, 1992, p461.

Chapter 4

A WALK IN THE PARADISE GARDEN

It has been said that death provides us with the perfect statistic: 1 in 1 die! Despite the fact that this prospect unites all humanity, we find it difficult to accept the death of someone close to us or the scenes of horrific carnage which frequently assault us from our TV screens. Death is a fact, but one that we would sooner not have to reckon with.

For the Christian, however, whilst the loss of a friend or family member brings natural grieving (even Jesus wept at the tomb of his friend Lazarus), our sense of loss and sadness is tempered by the belief that death is not the end. Those suffering loss are often comforted with the thought that the dead person has 'gone to heaven' or 'gone to be with the Lord'.

In a different context, evangelists sometimes try to use the belief in life after death to their advantage. By posing the question 'If you were to die tonight would you go to heaven or hell?' they seek to confront people with the importance of making a salvation decision before death. In so doing they imply that after death life goes on, and that the eternal destinies of heaven or hell are entered immediately.

But are these beliefs of instant comfort in heaven or instant torment in hell true to a biblical understanding of life after death?

LIFE GOES ON

The idea that there is a non-physical part of us which lives on after death was endorsed by Jesus when he said, 'Do not fear those who kill the body . . .' There is something about us which those who kill the body cannot touch.[1] Presumably it was this 'something' which John recognized in his vision as the souls of Christian martyrs living on in heaven after they had been killed.[2]

Sometimes this death-defying inner self is termed our soul (Gk *psyche*) and sometimes our 'spirit' (Gk *pneuma*). Jesus, at the point of physical death, committed his spirit into the care of his Father,[3] and the first Christian martyr, Stephen, as he faced his executioners cried out, 'Lord Jesus, receive my spirit' (*pneuma*).[4] Both Stephen and Jesus were clearly expecting a part of themselves to pass into God's presence at the point of their death.

However, although they both committed their *spirits* into God's keeping, the words 'soul' and 'spirit' are not used in the Bible to define completely separate aspects of our humanity; they are often interchangeable. We may think of ourselves as comprising three hermetically sealed units (body, soul, spirit), but figuring out exactly where spirit starts and soul ends is not something the Bible ever tries to do. It may be generally true that our spirit is our inner self in relationship with God, and our soul is our inner self in relationship to others, but even there the distinctions are blurred.

What is crystal clear is that humanity is only fully alive when body and soul/spirit are intact. The state of existence which our soul/spirit enters after the death of its body is 'provisional, temporary and incomplete' (Anthony Hoekema).[5] Jesus on the cross committed his spirit to his Father's care, but living on 'spiritually' was not to be his ultimate destiny. Three days of disembodied existence were enough! Physical resurrection was his goal, and that physical resurrection is held up by Paul as an example of what God intends for all of us.[6]

To put it plainly, 'the central message of scripture about the future of man is that of the resurrection body' (Hoekema).[7] The Christian hope is not to float eternally around heaven in the spiritual state we enter at death (wonderful though that experience will be) but to be recreated as a whole person – body, soul and spirit – on the renewed earth. Anything less, however wonderful, is 'provisional, temporary and incomplete'.

WHERE DO WE GO FROM HERE?

Having established that our soul/spirit lives on and enters heaven[8] through death, it may be interesting to examine a little more of what the Bible has to say about that temporary state between physical death and physical resurrection.

The Old Testament is quite clear that departed souls go to 'Sheol'. Much confusion has arisen about the afterlife due to the King James version of the Bible commonly translating 'Sheol' as 'hell'. This is unhelpful since 'Sheol' and 'hell' are two completely different destinations.

'Hell' (as we shall see) is a New Testament word for the place of final fiery judgement of Satan, his angels and all the unrighteous. Jesus warned that on Judgement Day the unrighteous will hear the terrible words, 'Depart from me, you who are cursed, into the eternal fire prepared for the devil and his angels'.[9]

'Sheol', on the other hand, is an Old Testament word meaning simply the 'realm of the dead'. It was not a place of punishment nor of reward, but of waiting. It was a world of spiritual existence which all (righteous and unrighteous) entered on their death. The New International Version captures the sense of Sheol better than the Authorized Version by translating the word as 'grave' rather than 'hell'. All die and all enter 'the grave' (Sheol).

However, even in the Old Testament it is possible to see the beginnings of an after-death distinction being made between those who enter death (Sheol) as righteous servants of God and those who enter death as unrighteous God-rejecters. At least two passages in the psalms indicate that whereas the unrighteous will be eternally imprisoned in Sheol, God will not leave his righteous servants in the realms of the dead for ever.

> Like sheep they [the foolhardy] are appointed for Sheol;
> Death shall be their shepherd;

straight to the grave they descend, and their form shall
    waste away; Sheol shall be their home.
But God will ransom my soul from the power of Sheol,
    for he will receive me.[10]

Therefore my heart is glad, and my soul rejoices; my
    body also rests secure.
For you do not give me up to Sheol, or let your faithful
    one see the Pit.

You show me the path to life.[11]

FROM SHEOL TO HADES

It is fascinating that on the day of Pentecost, when Peter is
preaching in the streets of Jerusalem, he quotes the above
passage from Psalm 16 as a way of explaining the resurrection
of Jesus. Peter implies that David was writing prophetically of
Jesus, and although through crucifixion Jesus had entered the
world of the dead 'he was not abandoned to Hades, nor did his
flesh experience corruption'.[12] God showed Jesus the 'path of
life' out of 'the grave'.

Peter's use of Psalm 16 thus bridges a gap between Old and
New Testaments, and it is interesting to note that where the
psalmist uses the Hebrew word 'Sheol', Peter substitutes the
Greek word 'Hades'. Hades is correctly understood as the New
Testament 'Sheol', that is 'the place of the departed', not 'hell'.
Sadly, meanings have once again been blurred by earlier ver-
sions of the Bible translating Hades as 'hell'. For example,
Jesus' words to Peter in Matthew 16 have a completely different
shade of meaning if Hades is understood correctly as 'death'
rather than incorrectly as 'hell'.

What Jesus actually said was 'I tell you, you are Peter, and on
this rock I will build my church, and the gates of Hades will not
prevail against it'.[13] Older translations (and recent songwriters)
have translated 'Hades' as 'hell' and have thus made Jesus say
that 'the gates of *hell* will not prevail against it'.

Translating 'Hades' as 'hell' conjures up lurid pictures of

demonic hosts waging war against the church from inside a gated city, with the church – acting on Jesus' authority – powerfully bursting those gates open. (Although why the church should want to break into hell has never been explained to me!) Whilst it is true that the church wages war against spiritual heavenly opposition,[14] Jesus is not talking about that in this passage.

What he is trying to explain to the newly commissioned 'rock', Peter, is that the church which he is going to play such a major role in establishing will not be limited by the death of either its founder (Jesus) or its apostles, because death cannot hold back the mission of Jesus through the church. Nor can it hold on to dead saints in Hades. 'The 'gates' of Hades (death) will open and allow first Jesus, and ultimately all believers, back into the realm of the living.

> To say that the powers of death shall not prevail against the church is thus to say that it will not die, and be shut in by the gates of death. The words do not indicate an attack by the 'powers of evil', but simply the process of death . . . Peter is to be the foundation stone of Jesus' new community of the restored people of God, a community which will last for ever (Dick France).[15]

Hades then, like Sheol in the Old Testament, is the realm of the dead. It is a realm to which Jesus holds the keys,[16] and eventually it will give up its dead so that all may stand, clothed in resurrection bodies, before God to face judgement.[17]

Finally, Hades itself will be destroyed, since the new humanity on the renewed earth will live for ever and so will have no need of its facilities![18]

DEVELOPING HADES

There is, however, one important development in the New Testament concept of Hades, which was missing from the Old Testament Sheol. During the period between the Testaments a belief had become popular in Judaism that there was a 'spatial separation in the underworld between the godly and the ungodly' (Anthony Hoekema).[19] In other words, the realm of the dead, whilst welcoming all – both good and bad – into its heavenly (ie spiritual) kingdom, now in some way kept the good apart from the bad.

'In Judaism there emerges a distinct doctrine of Sheol as a place of blessedness for the righteous but a place of suffering for the unrighteous' (George Eldon Ladd).[20] This belief was certainly prevalent in Jesus' time and well on into the next century. Josephus, a non-Christian first-century Jewish historian, debated the nature of the afterlife at some length with the Greek philosophers of his day, and his writings give a vivid insight into the Jewish view of Hades as a place where the spirits of the righteous experienced joy and those of the unrighteous suffering.

Josephus writes of Hades as a place 'wherein the souls of the righteous and the unrighteous are detained'. However, although the just and the unjust are both there, the just are not to be found 'in the same place wherein the unjust are confined'; once through the gate of death the just and the unjust souls are led to walk different paths by angels allotted to guide them.

Josephus continues, 'The just are guided to the right . . . and are led with hymns, sung by the angels appointed over that place, unto a region of light.' In this region 'there is no place of toil, no burning heat, no piercing cold – nor are any briars there'.

This place of blessing, rest and contentment is in sharp contrast to the fate of the unjust dead who, according to Josephus, having entered the gate 'are dragged by force to the left . . . by the angels allotted for punishment, no longer going with a good will, but as prisoners driven by violence'. These angels 'drag them into the neighbourhood of hell itself', and leave them where they 'continually hear the noise of it, and do not stand clear of the hot vapour itself'. Not surprisingly, 'when they have a near view of this spectacle, as of a terrible and exceeding great prospect of fire, they are struck with a fearful expectation of a future judgement and in effect punished thereby'. This sense of fearful foreboding is magnified as 'they see the place of the fathers and of the just' but cannot cross to them because a gulf 'deep and large is fixed between them' (Josephus).[21]

We can see from this graphic description of Hades a clear development in Jewish thought from a non-judgemental after-death waiting room (Sheol) to a place where final judgement is already fixed and indeed anticipated by the inhabitants. Each person, realizing their eternal fate, lives an intermediate spiritual existence already tasting blessing or pain.

That this belief was widespread in Judaism is clear but was it accepted by Jesus and taught by the apostles?

FROM HERE TO ETERNITY

As we have seen, there is no doubt that Jesus and the apostles believed that at the point of death the spirit lived on. Jesus consoled the thief on the cross by assuring him that his faith would merit him a place with Jesus in Paradise that very day.[22]

The word 'Paradise' introduces a very important new insight to our understanding of life in the world of the dead. Paradise literally means 'garden' and just as Hades (the world of departed spirits) is a part of heaven (the whole spirit world), so Paradise appears to be that part of Hades in which the departed souls of the righteous enjoy the presence of Jesus in the period between their death and resurrection to their new earthly home.

Jesus seems to imply that the thief, immediately after his death, will be conscious of Jesus' presence in the Paradise region of Hades.

Immediate post-death transition to Jesus' presence was also anticipated by Paul in Philippians 1. In struggling with the issue of his death, Paul's train of thought aroused two conflicting hopes within him. On the one hand, he reasoned, if he remained alive he would be able to continue his fruitful ministry to the gentiles and support the new churches he had started. On the other hand, for Paul facing death was not defeat or despair but 'gain' because, he said, he longed to 'depart and be with Christ, for that is far better'.

Similarly, in 2 Corinthians 5:1–6, Paul compares the relative merits of being 'at home in the body', which he describes as 'this earthly tent', and being 'at home with the Lord', 'clothed with our heavenly dwelling'. Opinions vary as to whether this 'heavenly building' or 'eternal house in heaven' refers to our spiritual state in Paradise with Jesus or to our resurrection body. In either case 'he [Paul] is very sure that if his earthly body should be dissolved in death, a blessed home beyond the grave awaits him' (R V G Tasker),[23] and that he would 'rather be away from the body and at home with the Lord'.[24]

The hope of both Jesus and Paul, then, was for continuing conscious existence after death, not in a shadowy 'world of the dead' but in Paradise. Knowing Jesus in Paradise, 'departing and being with Christ' or 'being at home with the Lord' all offer tremendous hope to the Christian as he or she passes through the doorway of death.

So we see a development of the concept of Hades in the New Testament. In some places it retains its general meaning of the 'whole world of the dead', but in other places it is used for that part of the world of the dead reserved for the unrighteous (the righteous being in Paradise). The development is seen most clearly in Jesus' story of Dives and Lazarus[25] who, after they die, are both very aware of their different surroundings in the afterlife. The wealthy Dives finds himself in a place of suffering, identified as Hades, whilst the poor Lazarus finds himself being comforted by Abraham – in a separate part of Hades. Both are in the world of the dead but a 'great chasm' is fixed between the place of Dives' suffering and the place of Lazarus' comfort.

How much is it reasonable to use the details of this story to debate the nature of life after death? Was Jesus using a well-known story simply to illustrate his teaching about the attitudes of rich people to poor people, or about God's attitude to both? Craig L Blomberg cautions that 'the fact that the source of much of the imagery of the parable probably was popular folklore should warn against viewing the details of this narrative as a realistic description of the afterlife'.[26]

Whilst allowing that the details of any parable can be pressed too far, it does seem unlikely that Jesus would use a story completely detached from reality to illustrate his points, particularly as those points relate directly to the eternal destinies of the characters in the story. So, with caution, it should still be possible to affirm that 'Jesus is here giving us a glimpse into the nature of the afterlife in the time between death and the final judgement'. As we study this 'glimpse' 'we see disembodied personalities who are very much aware of their condition of bliss or torment'. Yet 'both of them are in Hades' (Roger T Forster).[27]

This accords well with the conclusion of theologian Millard J Erickson that 'upon death believers go immediately to a place and condition of blessedness [in Paradise], and unbelievers to an experience of misery, torment and punishment'.[28]

David Watson, facing his own impending death, wrote, 'From the teaching of Jesus, it seems that at the moment of death there will be a great divide between those who know and love God and those who do not.' Those who do not know God will pass directly into Hades, knowing where they are and knowing where they are going. God's children, on the other hand, will enter that part of Hades (ie the world of the dead) which we call Paradise. Looking forward to being with Christ in Paradise, David Watson wrote, 'There will be a wonderful sense of being fully in God's presence, in an unspoilt and unbroken atmosphere of love, joy and praise.'[29]

The believer's direct entry into Paradise is interestingly hinted at by the experiences of those who have died and been resuscitated. David Watson again:

> Although it would be a mistake to base our beliefs on the experience of those who have clinically died but later have been restored to life, it is worth noting that of those who were Christians nearly all speak of walking into a garden full of staggeringly beautiful colours and exquisite music . . . so that it was with great reluctance that they came back to earth again.[30]

FEELING SLEEPY?

But if life between a believer's death and resurrection is a conscious experience of being with the Lord in the Paradise region of Hades, what about the claims of some that on death we simply 'fall asleep' and remain in spiritual suspended animation until Judgement Day and resurrection?

Certainly Paul used this terminology when encouraging the Thessalonian Christians not to become discouraged because some of their members had died before Jesus had returned. 'We do not want you to be ignorant about those who fall asleep,' he wrote. 'We believe that Jesus died and rose again and so we believe that God will bring with Jesus those who have fallen asleep in him'.[31] Whilst Paul affirms that those who have died have gone to be with Jesus (otherwise how could he bring them with him when he returns to judge the earth?) he appears to say that they are *sleeping* in heaven.

However, evidence from other New Testament passages seems to conflict with this. John hears the souls of the martyrs in heaven not snoring but shouting.[32] And, as we have seen, Jesus and Paul both anticipated *conscious* fellowship in heaven after death, Jesus with the thief on the cross and Paul with Jesus himself.

So if the New Testament reveals souls alive, conversing – shouting even! – and enjoying one another's company, then where does the idea of 'soul-sleep' fit in? Sleep sounds far too passive to permit all of this post-death spiritual activity! We need not be confused. Quite simply, 'sleep was a common term for death both in Greek and Hebrew literature and need not carry any theological significance' (George Eldon Ladd).[33] 'He has fallen asleep' is just another way of saying 'he has died' and tells us nothing about the state of those in that condition.

AND SO TO HELL

Traditionally, many Christians have believed that on dying human beings would either be welcomed in heaven or consigned to hell but, as we have seen, this belief does not do justice to the biblical view of life after death. Heaven refers to the whole world of spiritual reality not just our eternal home,[34] and the words 'Hades' and 'Sheol', which have often been translated 'hell', actually relate to our temporary spiritual home between death and resurrection rather than our eternal destiny after judgement. (Although, as we have seen, final judgement is anticipated in Hades because the righteous already enjoy being with Jesus in 'God's garden', Paradise, and the unrighteous are aware that they are eternally lost.)

So where does hell fit in? The word which is rightly translated 'hell' in the New Testament is the word 'Gehenna'. Gehenna was a real place, a valley lying to the south of Jerusalem, which in the Old Testament was called the 'Valley of Hinnom'. It had an evil reputation from the days when children were sacrificed there[35] and was synonymous with horror and judgement. In Jesus' day it was the place where the rubbish of Jerusalem was burned up. Jesus himself used the graphic imagery of the smouldering rubbish heap, and its associations with gross wickedness and God's judgement, as a picture of the fate awaiting the wicked on the final day. Hell (Gehenna) thus became the symbol *par excellence* of the place of final torment and destruction for the unrighteous.

Hell's fire was primarily prepared to punish Satan and his angels, but it will also consume those who are declared guilty on the Day of Judgement.[36]

Perhaps the most common misunderstanding about hell is the belief that many 'go to hell when they die'. According to the Bible hell is to do with *final* judgement. After our death we enter Paradise (Christians) or Hades (non-Christians) and there await physical resurrection, final judgement and eternal rewards (for the righteous a welcome into life on the new earth, for the unrighteous – humans and angels – the destructive fire of hell). Hades and Paradise are temporary, the new earth and hell are for ever. Hades and Paradise are getting fuller every day, but no one as yet has entered hell.

This is not the place to enter into debate about the nature of hell fire, that is whether the unrighteous will suffer torment eternally or be destroyed in the fire of hell; whether the purpose of hell is eternal judg*ing* (endlessly being punished for sin) or eternal judge*ment* (being judged guilty and condemned to destruction by an eternal, irrevocable decision of God). Whichever view one holds, it is undeniably true that the state of eternal suffering and the state of eternal destruction are both ghastly compared to the glorious, indescribably beautiful existence to be enjoyed by redeemed humanity on a renewed earth. Why dwell on comparing the relative 'merits'(!) of destruction with those of eternal torment (as some do)? When either view of hell is compared with eternal life, joy, peace, freedom, happiness, health and fulfilment, there really is only one choice.

It should be noted that hell as eternal torment and hell as eternal destruction are the only two views that the New Testament allow us. The rather silly claim of some that 'heaven will be boring' and 'I'd sooner be having a good time in hell' should make us all shudder with horror at where such ignorance is leading.

JUST PICTURE IT!

In conclusion, it might be helpful to represent what the Bible teaches about our after-death experience in diagram form (see next page). I hope the detail in this chapter has not obscured the main objective which is to demonstrate that the spiritual existence we enter at death is not permanent. For a while we will be in heaven, but the believer, revelling in the beauty of heaven's Paradise garden, can still say that the best is yet to be! Until our resurrection we shall never be fully human, and until the earth is renewed we shall never feel fully at home.

NOTES ON CHAPTER 4

1   Matthew 10:28.
2   Revelation 6:9–10.
3   Luke 23:46.
4   Acts 7:59.

Old Testament

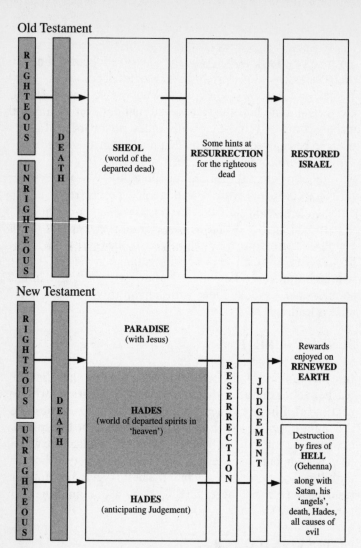

RIGHTEOUS		
UNRIGHTEOUS	DEATH	**SHEOL** (world of the departed dead)

Some hints at **RESURRECTION** for the righteous dead

RESTORED ISRAEL

New Testament

RIGHTEOUS		**PARADISE** (with Jesus)
UNRIGHTEOUS	DEATH	**HADES** (world of departed spirits in 'heaven')
		HADES (anticipating Judgement)

RESERRECTION

JUDGEMENT

Rewards enjoyed on **RENEWED EARTH**

Destruction by fires of **HELL** (Gehenna) along with Satan, his 'angels', death, Hades, all causes of evil

N.B. Hades is sometimes used as a general word for the whole 'world of the dead' (including Paradise) and sometimes used, as in the diagram above, as the after-death waiting place of the unrighteous.

5   Anthony A Hoekema, *The Bible and the future*, Paternoster Press, 1979, p95.
6   1 Corinthians 15:20–23.
7   *The Bible and the future*, see above, p91.
8   References to heaven in this book should always be taken to mean the 'invisible spiritual world where God lives'.
9   Matthew 25:41 (NIV).
10 Psalm 49:14,15.
11 Psalm 16:9–11.
12 Acts 2:31.
13 Matthew 16:18.
14 See chapter three.
15 R T France, *The Gospel according to Matthew*, Tyndale New Testament Commentaries, Inter-Varsity Press, 1986, p255.
16 Revelation 1:18.
17 Revelation 20:13.
18 Revelation 20:14.
19 *The Bible and the future*, see above, p99.
20 George Eldon Ladd, *Theology of the New Testament*, Lutterworth Press, 1975, p194.
21 Josephus, 'A discourse to the Greeks concerning Hades'.
22 Luke 23:42,43.
23 R V G Tasker, *2 Corinthians*, Inter-Varsity Press, p81.
24 2 Corinthians 5:8.
25 Luke 16:19–31.
26 Craig L Blomberg, *Interpreting the parables*, Apollos, 1990, p206.
27 Roger T Forster, *Eternal destiny: heaven and hell*, Ichthus Christian Fellowship, p19.
28 Millard J Erickson, *Christian theology*, Marshall Pickering, p1183.
29 David Watson, *Fear no evil*, Hodder & Stoughton, 1984, p164.
30 *Fear no evil*, see above.
31 1 Thessalonians 4:13,14, (NIV).
32 Revelation 6:9–10.

33 *Theology of the New Testament*, see above, p554.
34 See chapter three.
35 2 Kings 16:3; 23:10.
36 Matthew 25:41.

Chapter 5

LET'S GET PHYSICAL

At the end of the last chapter we left our departed Christian spirits in the Paradise district of Hades, enjoying life with Jesus but still experiencing a sense of incompleteness. For all the pleasures of Paradise, we were never designed to live in a spirit world. The best is yet to come and the residents of Paradise, secure in God's promise of new heavens and a new earth, hopefully await the day when spirit and body will be reunited to enjoy life on the new earth. As the song says, 'Everybody needs some body'!

If our eternal destination was heaven then a new body would be unnecessary since, as we have seen, spirits are quite capable of enjoying heaven. The promise of a new earth, however, makes sense of the promise of bodily resurrection since our new physical bodies will need a new earth to live on. It is strange how many Christians claim to believe in physical resurrection whilst still entertaining notions of a 'spiritual' heaven being their eternal home. Here again, in our hope for resurrection, we see evidence that 'the destiny of the cosmos is not an ethereal "heaven", but a re-created universe' (John Stott).[1]

But what will our resurrection bodies be like? Will we look the same? And will they indeed be 'physical' – doesn't Paul say that we will have 'spiritual bodies'?[2]

What about people who have been cremated or lost at sea – what will resurrection mean for them? Answers to these and other questions form the subject matter of this chapter.

THE IMPORTANCE OF RESURRECTION

Anyone who has read the New Testament can surely be in no doubt that the theme of resurrection is played frequently and loudly.

After faithfully waiting for the gift of the Holy Spirit at Pentecost, Peter grasped the opportunity aroused by the disciples' spirit-filled hubbub to explain to the watching crowd what was going on. In his address he quickly deals with the Holy Spirit's role in their behaviour[3] and moves on to talk about the recently executed Jesus.[4] The cross, however, is not what is uppermost in Peter's mind because the majority of the rest of his sermon is taken up with the fact that God has raised Jesus up, 'having freed him from death, because it was impossible for him to be held in its power'.[5] In relative terms, Peter spends far longer explaining the facts of Jesus' resurrection than he does speaking about his crucifixion.

From this point on, the resurrection of Jesus is at the heart of the message preached by the apostles. A few days later the Sadducees (who did not believe in any kind of resurrection) were upset and 'came to them, much annoyed because they [Peter and John] were teaching the people and proclaiming that in Jesus there is the resurrection of the dead'.[6] This official disapproval did nothing to dampen the zeal of the apostles, and wherever they went they continued to preach Jesus crucified but resurrected and very much alive!

In fact this excitement about Jesus' resurrection inspired the apostles to great boldness in witnessing. After all, they knew that Jesus was with them. He was not dead but alive, raised from the world of the dead by his heavenly Father. What had they to fear by giving everything to serve a living God who was so powerful?

Whilst the disciples were celebrating and preaching the resurrection, Saul the Pharisee was executing plans to destroy this unwholesome Jewish sect of followers of Jesus. By no means convinced of Jesus' resurrection, no one was more surprised than he to encounter the living Jesus on the Damascus Road![7]

This personal encounter with the resurrected Christ transformed Paul's life and formed the basis for his future ministry.[8]

Indeed, so convinced did he become of the resurrection of Jesus and its implications for all Jesus' followers that he was to write, 'If Christ has not been raised, your faith is futile and you are still in your sins. Then those also who have died in Christ have perished. If for this life only we have hoped in Christ, we are of all people most to be pitied. But, in fact, Christ has been raised from the dead . . .'[9] Earlier in the same chapter, Paul told the Corinthians that the crucifixion and the resurrection of Jesus were of 'first importance' and together formed the basis of their faith in God.

The resurrection of Jesus was therefore a (if not *the*) central theme in the apostles' good news. It meant that Jesus was demonstrably the Son of God, that God's power was proved to be greater than Satan's, and that Jesus could be known as a personal friend and companion. But alongside this joyful proclamation of 'Jesus is alive' ran a parallel hope for the future: the hope of resurrection for all believers in Jesus Christ.

Far from being a one-off event, the resurrection of Jesus proved that death could be overcome by everyone. Death had ceased to be the ultimate destination and had become instead merely a staging post on the journey from this age to the age to come. Jesus was seen as the 'first fruits of those who have died' and as the 'firstborn within a large family'.[10] All believers were one day expected to experience the awesome re-creative power of God restoring their spirits to a bodily existence.

This is the Christian hope. Not a Hindu-like hope of reincarnation after death, either as a higher life form (if we have been good this time around) or as a pig or slug (if we have not). Not a Buddhist-like hope of floating off into spiritual nothingness when we die. Certainly not an atheist humanist's despairing belief in complete obliteration at death. Our hope is for eternal life in a resurrected body on a re-created earth. Their firm belief in resurrection inspired the first Christians to face death with a confidence that onlookers must have found startling; our belief should continue to do the same for us today.

JESUS AND RESURRECTION

As we have seen, the believer's hope of future bodily resurrection is inextricably linked to Jesus' resurrection. Indeed, Jesus himself went so far as to say, '*I am* the resurrection and the life. Those who believe in me, even though they die, will live, and everyone who lives and believes in me will never die.'[11] Resurrection leading to eternal life is thus the privilege of those who believe in Jesus. 'The resurrection of Jesus provides solid, visible, tangible, public evidence of God's purpose to . . . give us new bodies in a new world' (John Stott).[12]

Because of Jesus' mastery over death, he is not only the one who 'was dead' but now is 'alive for ever and ever',[13] he is also the one who now holds the 'keys of Death and of Hades'. The world of the dead is pictured as having gates which are normally kept locked so that once departed spirits have passed through they have no way back to the land of the living. Jesus, however, inspires hope by letting us know that he holds the keys to those gates. He alone can unlock death's gates, release departed spirits out of Hades[14] and rejoin them with a physical body.

So Jesus' resurrection provides the evidence that resurrection is possible and the hope-promise that we can share in this great reversal of death. 'What happened to Jesus is understood as the dawn and assured promise of the coming glory of God over all, as the victory of life from God over death' (Jurgen Moltmann).[15] Marvellous though this resurrection hope is, it still begs the question, what will our resurrection bodies be like? What clues does the Bible give us?

IT IS I, ME, MYSELF

There can be no doubt that the figure who met with the disciples in the upper room, walked with the two men on the road to Emmaus and ate fish with the fishermen *was* Jesus.[16] Patiently he revealed his true identity to friends and disciples who were just coming to terms with losing him. Teaching them about his own resurrection, showing them the scar marks on his body, talking with them at some length to prove beyond doubt that it was really him – it must have been a spooky experience for them. If a close friend of mine died, and a week after his funeral somebody who looked like him suddenly appeared and tried to persuade me that he was the very friend I had watched being buried, whatever the physical similarities I would have my doubts and take some convincing! Small wonder that the disciples 'thought that they were seeing a ghost'. Jesus' words were reassuring and alarming at the same time! 'Look at my hands and feet; see that it is I myself. Touch me and see; for a ghost does not have flesh and bones as you see that I have.'[17]

Jesus after resurrection was the same person as Jesus before death. It was he, himself. The same will be true for us: 'It is not as disembodied spirits that God promises us eternal life, but as personalities expressed in a new kind of body . . . Just as a message is still the same message, whether it is spoken in words or flashed in Morse code, so, according to the Bible, we shall be the same persons, whatever the material form in which our personalities may be expressed' (Professor Donald Mackay).[18]

A RE-CREATED BODY

One of the big questions to address is, will God somehow reclothe my existing skeleton in order to resurrect me, or will he remake everything from scratch? What raw materials does God require to perform the act of resurrection?

Jesus resuscitated dead corpses several times. Lazarus, Jairus' daughter and the widow of Nain's son were all 'clinically dead' but restored to life by Jesus.[19] However, the life that they were brought back to was life on this earth and eventually, like all human beings, they died. Their 'new' body was simply their old body rejoined with their spirit and it was still subject to decay, illness, wear and tear and, eventually, death.

We must remember (and rejoice) in the fact that it is Jesus and not Lazarus who gives us the pattern for resurrection. When Jesus' spirit was brought out of the world of the dead by the power of God and rejoined with a human body, it was by an act of re-creation not resuscitation. 'The resurrection was a dramatic act of God by which he arrested the natural process of decay and decomposition ("you will not let your holy one see decay"), rescued Jesus out of Hades, and changed his body into a new vehicle for his personality, endowed with new powers and possessing immortality' (John Stott).[20]

Jesus was not so much reborn as re-created. His new body was in many respects probably very similar to his old one to look at. Certainly it was re-created with the identifying scars which were to impress the suspicious Thomas.[21] For us too 'in giving us new bodies, there will be continuity without the suggestion of absolute physical identity. God does not need to search for the same atoms and molecules that once constituted us; if he did, there wouldn't be nearly enough to go around, since we all wear second hand clothes in that respect . . . Any resurrection to physical life will involve a massive act of new creation' (Tom Wright).[22]

Those who (understandably) worry about the possibility of resurrection after cremation, for example, on the grounds that there is no body left to raise, are thus reassured. God is more than capable of re-creating a suitable body for every spirit that needs one!

A SUITABLE BODY

Why will God re-create rather than simply resuscitate? Possibly because the environment of the new earth, itself redeemed and renewed, swept clean of evil and harm, will be an alien environment to us. Our bodies, although designed for a perfect pre-fallen world, are now adapted to life in a fallen one. We have developed almost miraculous innate abilities which enable us to fight disease, live in harsh climates and cope with emotional stress.

However, God's promise is that the spiritual, environmental and emotional brokenness which forms our normal daily surroundings will be mended in the age to come. Our new bodies will be bodies that are equipped for the new environment and atmosphere of glory-on-earth.

Paul touched on this in his teaching on resurrection in 1 Corinthians 15. He points out that even in this current age 'not all flesh is alike, but there is one flesh for human beings, another for animals, another for birds and another for fish'. God has already provided different bodies adapted to the needs of different environments. A bird's body is uniquely created for the demands of flight, whereas a fish's body is purpose-built for life under water. The idea of the two exchanging their habitats is laughable (to everyone except a macroevolutionist!). Paul implies that it would be equally laughable to imagine that resurrection will just be a case of bringing this body back to life to live in the age to come, because the 'perishable' can no more inherit the 'imperishable' than a cod can inherit a robin's nest.

So, resurrected 'with what kind of body? As with Christ, the same yet not the same; this body, but adapted to the new conditions of heavenly existence' (Gordon Fee).[23]

C S Lewis in his visionary book, *The great divorce*, paints the following picture of renewed humanity living together in the 'foothills of heaven':

> I saw people coming to meet us. Because they were bright I saw them while they were still very distant, and at first I did not know that they were people at all . . . The earth shook under their tread as their strong feet sank into the wet turf. A tiny haze and a sweet smell went up where they crushed the grass and scattered the dew. Some were naked, some robed. But the naked ones did not seem less adorned, and the robes did not disguise in those who wore them the massive grandeur of muscle and the radiant smoothness of flesh. Some were bearded but no one in that company struck me as being of any particular age.

One gets glimpses, even in our country, of that which is ageless – heavy thought in the face of an infant, and a frolic childhood in that of a very old man. Here it was all like that.[24]

In this lovely vision C S Lewis pictures humanity recognizable as such and acting as such, but magnificently adapted to the life of eternity. His imagery manages to hold together pictures of recognizable, renewed human forms with hints of the 'otherness' which will surely mark life on the new earth. He introduces another question that is frequently asked about our resurrection body, namely, will we all be the same age?' It is difficult to imagine what the concept of 'age' will mean in eternity. It seems possible that C S Lewis with his description of agelessness comes near to the truth. Since there will be no growing old in the age to come, whatever state we are resurrected into will be the one in which we spend eternity. It may be that people whose bodies never fully developed in this age, for example children who died, people who were aborted as foetuses or adults who were deformed by disease, will be gloriously gifted with the sort of perfect body that evil robbed them of previously. Certainly those of us who struggle with varying kinds and degrees of disability in this age will enjoy the very same freedom from the 'bondage to decay'[25] which creation itself looks forward to. No more arthritic joints, wheezy chests or ringing ears. The old has gone and the new has come, and, in a life that goes on for ever, wondering about someone's age will be rather pointless!

Jesus in his resurrection was granted a new body with which to enjoy eternity.[26] He 'was transformed, living on the new, eternal, glorious level of the age to come. *That* Jesus is the pattern for the resurrection of his people. Not less real but more real' (Stephen Travis).[27]

A SPIRITUAL BODY

Some at this point may be hanging their heads and tutting at this author's naivety! After all, surely Paul knocks all this crass literalism on the head when he talks of our resurrection bodies as being 'spiritual bodies'.[28] Was it not therefore his view that resurrection bodies would be altogether more ethereal and transparent? And anyway, didn't Jesus himself say that 'in the resurrection they . . . are like angels in heaven'?[29] If 'spiritual angels' are our prototype for resurrection, we need to radically rethink all that we have affirmed so far in this chapter! Let us look at each passage in turn.

We shall discuss Jesus' statement that we shall be like angels in the next chapter, but what does Paul mean by describing our resurrection body as 'spiritual'? 'Spiritual' is an adjective that Paul used several times in his epistles. He wrote of spiritual gifts, spiritual people, spiritual blessings and spiritual songs.[30] Does he mean that these are ghostly things, somehow made of 'spirit'? Surely not. Paul uses the word 'spirit' in contrast to 'flesh' (ie our fallen nature) not in contrast to our bodies, so what he means is that each of the above is filled by the Spirit and guided by the Spirit – spiritual gifts being *given* by the Spirit, a spiritual person being someone who is *filled with* and *guided by* the Spirit, and so on.

To follow this train of thought, the resurrection body is ' "spiritual" not in the sense of "immaterial" but of "supernatural" . . . The transformed body, therefore, is not composed of "spirit"; it is a *body* adapted to the eschatological existence that is under the ultimate domination of the Spirit' (Gordon Fee).[31] So, here again, Paul infers that our resurrection is going to be so much more than a simple 'reanimation of corpses'; rather it will provide us with 'a new body, animated by the Spirit of God' (C K Barrett).[32]

Wonderful! For the first time ever we will be truly equipped to 'walk in the Spirit'. Just as all of us who suffer from physical weakness will know release in the age to come, others of us who daily hunger to be filled more fully with the Spirit of God will, for the first time ever, be filled to overflowing. Indeed, Paul himself writes that in this age we have only an initial down payment on the fullness of the Spirit that we shall enjoy on the new earth in our resurrection bodies. Spirit-filled and Spirit-led

– it is in this sense that our resurrection bodies will be 'spiritual'.

TOO GOOD TO BURN?

So far we have been talking of the wonderful bodies that God will re-create for us to live in on the new earth in the age to come. Bodies that are like Jesus' resurrection body, totally suited to the life of the future and totally filled and guided by the Holy Spirit. Suitable bodies. Spiritual bodies. We have seen that for all those who believe in him Jesus becomes the resurrection and the life.[33] But what of those who do not believe? What of those who are numbered amongst the unrighteous unbelievers on Judgement Day, those whose spirits currently languish in that part of Hades separated from the Paradise garden by a huge, uncrossable gulf?

Some passages[34] do seem to imply that it is only the righteous who enjoy resurrection and that the rest (presumably) just stay in a kind of doleful suspended inanimation for the rest of eternity. There are several problems with this view, chiefly that Hades itself is going to be destroyed when the new earth is created.[35] This leaves the unrighteous departed spirits all undressed with no place to go!

However, other texts help us clarify that both righteous *and* unrighteous will be resurrected. This is made clear in numerous passages in both the Old and New Testaments. Daniel 12:2, for example, declares, 'Many of those who sleep in the dust of the earth shall awake, some to everlasting life, and some to shame and everlasting contempt.' Jesus himself plainly teaches that 'the hour is coming when all who are in their graves will hear his voice and will come out – those who have done good, to the resurrection of life, and those who have done evil, to the resurrection of condemnation'.[36] It is this 'resurrection of condemnation' which the 'goats' receive in Jesus' story of the sheep and the goats,[37] and it is this terrible resurrection that leads via judgement to the destructive flames of hell, the prospect of which so troubles the spirits of the unrighteous departed in Hades.

How great is God's love that, without our even asking and before we were even born, he sent his Son to endure our deserved punishment, so that simply because of our faith in him now we can rejoice in the splendid prospect of resurrection *and life* in the age to come.

TRANSFORMATION OF THE LIVING

We have seen that both the faithful and the faithless will be called back through the gates of death, the former to inherit the eternal life on earth that they had already begun to anticipate in Hades' Paradise garden and the latter to bear the eternal punishment for their rejection of God in this life. For the sake of completeness we ought to ask, what about those who are still alive on the earth at the time of Jesus' return? Will they just carry on regardless into the age to come?

By no means. It would be impossible. As we have already seen, the bodies that they will be living in will be suited to this age; the purified atmosphere of eternity will require them to inherit new powers and properties. 'Flesh and blood cannot inherit the kingdom of God, nor does the perishable inherit the imperishable.'[38]

For those who are alive, transformation is just as necessary as for those who are dead. The journey through the gates of death into Hades and back will not be required of those alive at that time, but they will enjoy an instant renewal of being which transforms their body into one suitable for the age to come. 'In a twinkling of an eye', the living believer's decaying and dying body will be clothed with 'imperishability and immortality'.[39]

When he returns Jesus will 'change these wretched bodies of ours so that they resemble his own glorious body, by that power of his which makes him in command of everything'.[40] As the world comes back under the absolute dominion of its one true Lord, and as creation itself is reborn, we shall be physically reformed to enjoy its splendours, delight in one another and worship its Creator!

NOTES ON CHAPTER 5

1 John Stott, *The contemporary Christian*, Inter-Varsity Press, 1992, p85.
2 1 Corinthians 15:44.
3 Acts 2:14–21.
4 Acts 2:22–23.
5 Acts 2:24–32.
6 Acts 4:1–2.
7 Acts 9:3–7.
8 Eg Galatians 1:11–12,14–17.
9 1 Corinthians 15:17–20.
10 1 Corinthians 15:20; Romans 8:29.
11 John 11:25–26.
12 *The contemporary Christian*, see above, p81.
13 Revelation 1:18.
14 See chapter four.
15 Jurgen Moltmann, *Theology of hope*, SCM Press, 1969, p201.
16 Luke 24:36.
17 Luke 24:37–39.
18 From David Watson, *Fear no evil*, Hodder & Stoughton, 1984, p163.
19 John 11; Mark 5:21–43; Luke 7:11–15.
20 *The contemporary Christian*, see above, p76.
21 John 20:27,28.
22 N T Wright, Drew lecture, 1993, used with permission.
23 Gordon D Fee, *First epistle to the Corinthians*, Wm B Eerdmans Publishing Co (US), 1987, p777.
24 C S Lewis, *The great divorce*, Fontana (HarperCollins Publishers), 1971, p29.
25 Romans 8:21.
26 Whilst the resurrection of Jesus in a physical body gives substance to our wonderful future hope, his subsequent ascension appears to confuse the issue. Two questions are raised. First, how can a physical Jesus enter the spiritual realm of the heavenly places? And second, is the ascension, like the resur-

rection, a pattern for believers? In other words, will we enter the heavenly places in our resurrection bodies as Jesus did?

First, we must always remember that Jesus is our pattern only up to a point. He was, and is, fully human (as we are) *and* fully God (as we are not and never shall be). Maybe *his* resurrection body had to be as capable of entering the heavenlies as walking the earth precisely because his divinity and humanity demanded both to be possible. The same demands are not placed on our humanity.

Second, whilst the New Testament clearly states more than once that Jesus' resurrection was a pattern for ours, nowhere is it stated that his ascension is a pattern for ours. Why? Because Jesus' post-resurrection destiny was to be the divine human King of heaven, whilst our post-resurrection destiny is to govern the earth on his behalf.

Space prevents extended discussion of the ascension, but for further stimulating thought on the order of existence that Jesus entered at his resurrection try reading chapter 16, 'Miracles of the New Creation', in C S Lewis' *Miracles – A preliminary study*, Fount (HarperCollins Publishers), 1993.

27 Stephen Travis, *I believe in the second coming of Jesus*, Hodder & Stoughton, 1988, p172.
28 1 Corinthians 15:44.
29 Matthew 22:30.
30 Romans 1:11; 1 Corinthians 2:15; Ephesians 1:3; Ephesians 5:19.
31 *First epistle to the Corinthians*, see above, p29.
32 C K Barrett, *First epistle to the Corinthians*, New Testament Commentaries, A & C Black, 1971, p373.
33 John 11:25–26.
34 Eg Luke 20:35.
35 Revelation 20:14.
36 John 5:28–29.
37 Matthew 25:31–46.
38 1 Corinthians 15:50.
39 1 Corinthians 15:51–53.
40 Philippians 3:21 (J B Phillips).

PART 2

VISIONS OF LIFE ON THE NEW EARTH

'. . . the earth will be full of the knowledge of the Lord
as the waters cover the sea.'

Isaiah 11:9

'Always teach provisionally, because only God knows
for sure!'

*From 'First rule of teaching', Murray Schaffer
(Canadian musicologist)*

Chapter 6

PERSON TO PERSON

The aim of this book has been to redefine biblically our future hope. Whereas many Christians have either no real view at all of what God has in store for those who love him, or a distorted image of a sort of spiritual never-never' land called heaven, the truth, as we have seen, is altogether more wonderful.

The future of the believer is inextricably bound up with the renewal of all things. God has promised a new earth as the inheritance of his people and what God has promised will surely come to pass. With G C Berkouwer, we affirm then that 'it is precisely ordinary earthly existence that is redeemed'.[1]

But what will it be like to be a redeemed, resurrected human being on God's new earth? Once one has biblically adjusted one's thinking to accommodate belief in an eternal *earthly* future a host of questions flood to mind. Will we recognize one another? Will there be animals there? Will we eat? Will we have to work?

Many Christians have fought shy of speculating about these questions, preferring to shelter behind the safety of uncontroversial statements such as 'We don't know what it will be like, but we do know that it will be incredibly wonderful'. That is true enough, and the sure knowledge that our God loves us reassures us that, whatever the future holds, it will be good. This comforting, if vague, optimism about our future is summed up well in these lines taken from a poem by Marie Luise Kaschnitz:

Do you believe they asked me
In a life after death
And I answered: Yes
But I could not explain
What it might look like
There

One thing only I knew
Not a hierarchy
Of saints sitting on golden thrones
Not a fall
Of damned souls
Only

Only love made free
Never exhausted
Flowing over me . . .

Do you not then, ask the questioners
Expect more after death?
And I answer
Not less[2]

An expectation that the future holds 'more not less' is wonderful but is this really all God permits us to know? Has he revealed in scripture anything at all which might give more substance to our future hope? Certainly the Bible does not have a block of chapters headed 'What life on the new earth will be like,' but it does give us innumerable clues. I concede that some of this chapter and the one that follows may lean towards speculation in attempting to piece together these biblical clues, but I am encouraged that 'speculation is a legitimate theological activity, as long as we are aware that we are speculating' (Millard J Erickson)![3]

Having admitted that what follows is speculative and visionary (in part) yet, I believe, nonetheless biblical for that, let us proceed to seek insight into God's future for us on planet New Earth.

CREATION REDEEMED

The world is beautiful. Compare the earth's surface with pictures of any other planet in our solar system and you are immediately aware of the rich variety of features which sets the earth apart as something unique. And yet, for all the wonder of earthly creation, we must recall that in its present form it is under God's curse because of humanity's rebellion.[4] It is a broken creation which, whilst still retaining enough of its Creator's 'fingerprints' to reveal his 'eternal power and divine nature', nevertheless is in this age 'subjected to futility' and in 'bondage to decay'.[5]

This malfunction in the fabric of the earth was clearly not God's intention since everything he saw before the Fall was 'very good'.[6] The marvellous prospect for us is that it is this 'very good' pre-Fall creation that God will renew at the return of Jesus Christ.

The Old Testament prophets envisioned this great climax to the age in passages like the following:

> For I am about to create new heavens and a new earth;
> the former things shall not be remembered or come to
> mind.
> But be glad and rejoice forever in what I am creating . . .
> I will rejoice in Jerusalem and delight in my people . . .
> They shall build houses and inhabit them; they shall
> plant vineyards and eat their fruit . . . and my
> chosen shall long enjoy the work of their hands . . .
> Before they call I will answer, while they are yet speaking
> I will hear.
> The wolf and the lamb shall feed together, the lion shall
> eat straw like the ox . . .
> They shall not hurt or destroy on all my holy mountain,
> says the Lord.[7]

Commenting on these verses, John D Watts observes, 'They point to God's original and ultimate plan for humanity in a totally non-violent and innocent creation.'[8] What a wonderful picture. A totally non-violent and innocent creation! This new earth sounds like it will be not only indescribably beautiful but fulfilling beyond our imagination.

Not only will every nook and cranny of life be cleansed of all trace of evil but so too will our memories since 'the former things shall not be remembered'. This cannot mean that after our resurrection we shall lose all recollection of our previous lives. After *his* resurrection Jesus still recognized friends and places that he had known, and he was still aware of who he was and what he had been through. Surely in his grace and mercy God will erase from our memories the 'former things' that have been abolished from life on the new earth, that is death, evil and suffering.

So we will remember and rejoice in the presence of redeemed brothers and sisters in Christ (see below), but not be tormented by memories of 'lost' unredeemed friends and relatives. We shall marvel at the beauty of creation without feeling guilty about the way we have abused it in this present age. The sinful and the evil will be 'former things' in that they will no longer exist and, praise God, we shall be saved not only from their presence but from their very memory.

Isaiah foresees a world of peace and harmony under God's Kingship. Incidentally, we should not be misled by the reference to God's 'holy mountain' as the scene of all this wonderful restoration. 'It is not that peace is restricted to one place but rather that a dramatic change has come over the whole earth. When the true order of creation is restored the whole earth is the Lord's hill, indwelt by his holiness . . . Everywhere God is present in holiness, and in every place the knowledge of him is enjoyed to its fullest extent' (Alec Motyer).[9]

REDEEMED RELATIONSHIPS

Pardon me, don't I know you?
Excuse me for stating the obvious, but the new earth will be full of people. People who have been deemed worthy, because of

Jesus' saving work and their personal faith in God, to share in this eternal fullness of life will enjoy relationship together. Louis Berkhof claims that 'there will be recognition and social intercourse on an elevated plane'.[10] Or, to put it more simply, we may well bump into people we recognize and we will get on perfectly with everyone!

Who will we relate to? Everyone that we meet.[11] Since we are to receive resurrection bodies it seems fair to assume that we shall not be omnipresent spirits. We shall live in one particular part of the earth as we do now and enjoy relationships mainly within a particular circle of people. It seems reasonable to believe that we shall certainly meet people we know and maybe bump into others we have heard of. Given that we are able to move about the new earth and that we shall be there for eternity, it may well be, for example, that in time we will meet many of the Bible characters or other Christian 'greats' who were saved by faith. Imagine bumping into Abraham, David, Peter or Paul and enjoying their company as equals in the grace of God. Imagine the thrill of passing the time of eternal day chatting with John Wesley, Charles Spurgeon or William Booth. Imagine the joy of resuming relationships which were special to us on this earth in the purified atmosphere of perfected heavenly love. Imagine answering the door and finding a long-lost friend or family member there.

Just take a moment to imagine. John Lennon urged us to 'imagine there's no heaven', but it's much more enjoyable imagining what the real heaven will be like!

Marriage made in heaven?
Many wonder about the nature of exclusive relationships – for example, between husband and wife – in the age to come. Jesus commented directly on this question when answering a question from the Sadducees. Their question, in a nutshell, was this. In the resurrection, to whom will a woman who has had several husbands in this age be married? Jesus' answer was 'in the resurrection they neither marry nor are given in marriage, but are like angels in heaven'.[12]

Apparently the exclusive and intimate marriage relationship is a thing to be enjoyed in this age only. The pleasure and fulfilment it affords will be transcended by the intensity of our union with God himself and the fulfilment of our relationships with one another. God's gift of sexual union will thus be no longer necessary either for reproduction (since like the angels we shall not reproduce, the earth already being filled with God's redeemed family) or for personal fulfilment. 'The exclusive sexual aspect of marriage . . . will be a thing of the past in God's new world of deeply satisfying relationships amongst all God's people' (Stephen Travis).[13]

This is not to say that I will not recognize my wife in heaven, nor that our relationship there will be less fulfilling than it is here but rather, in common with all of my relationships in the age to come, it will be 'not less but more'.

What about Jesus' statement that we shall be like angels? Some have taken this as teaching that in the age to come we shall be asexual, that is neither male nor female. The crux of the matter is what 'being like angels' in the resurrection amounts to.

Fortunately Luke appears to provide an explanation of what it means to be 'like angels' when he writes, 'Those who are considered worthy of a place in that age and in the resurrection from the dead . . . *cannot die any more, because they are like angels* . . .' [my italics].[14] To be like angels therefore means not that we shall be genderless but that we shall not die. With the abolition of death in the age to come, human life will not have to be reproduced and so sexual union will be unnecessary. Ben Witherington comments that being like an angel 'amounts to having a deathless but not necessarily a genderless existence',[15] a view endorsed by Anthony Hoekema who affirms that 'Jesus' teaching here does not imply that there will be no sex differences in the age to come'[16] but rather that marriage will be unnecessary both for reproduction and fulfilment; all of our relationships will reach a degree of perfection which would make even the best of marriages a poor second best.

All too often we see the future as 'God and me' in perfect harmony and pay no attention to the implications of living in a redeemed society. Walter Rauschenbusch parodies this view brilliantly by describing traditional views of heaven as a 'a throng of souls, an unorganized crowd of saints, who each carry a harp but have not even formed an orchestra'.[17] Far from suffering such unorganized individualism on the new earth, we shall instead be set free from inhibition, shyness and personal insecurities to relate openly and honestly with one another. With no deceit or mistrust clouding our spirits, we shall communicate and co-operate in the joyful openness that Adam and Eve must have experienced before the crippling effects of their rebellion spoiled everything.

Speaking of which . . .
In our redeemed relationships, how will we communicate? What language shall we speak? Once again we need to recall that a multilingual world was not God's intention. Different languages and the barrier they represent to human unity were a result of man's sin, a measure taken by God to ensure that 'all the descendants of Noah can no longer live together and co-operate on anti-God projects' (Gordon Wenham).[18]

This measure, however, is only temporal and the prophet Zephaniah looked forward to the age when God would undo the effects of Babel. 'At that time I will change the speech of the peoples to a pure speech, that all of them may call on the name of the Lord and serve him with one accord.'[19] Whether or not it will be the tongues of angels[20] that we shall all speak, this new language will enable all people to communicate freely and openly.

Nation to nation
The possibility of a common language uniting humanity on the new earth naturally leads us on to question the nature of international relationships in the age to come. In one sense, of course, we shall all be one united, holy nation, worshipping God in unity of spirit. However, many of the prophetic glimpses of the future seem to imply that nationhood will in some sense still exist, but without the negative overtones of

racial disharmony and suspicion which sadly mar intercultural relationships today.

> In days to come the mountain of the Lord's house
> shall be established as the highest of the mountains, and
>   shall be raised up above the hills.
> Peoples shall stream to it, and many nations shall come
>   and say:
> 'Come, let us go up to the mountain of the Lord, to the
>   house of the God of Jacob;
> that he may teach us his ways and that we may walk in
>   his paths.'
> For out of Zion shall go forth instruction, and the word
>   of the Lord from Jerusalem.
> He shall judge between many peoples, and shall arbitrate
>   between strong nations far away;
> they shall beat their swords into ploughshares, and their
>   spears into pruning hooks;
> nation shall not lift up sword against nation, neither shall
>   they learn war any more;
> but they shall all sit under their own vines and under their
>   own fig trees, and no one shall make them afraid; for
>   the mouth of the Lord of hosts has spoken.[21]

This prophetic passage, if taken as having end-time relevance, seems to indicate that separate national identities and cultural differences may well exist (but without the divisiveness inherent in them in this age). The nations, whilst retaining a rich diversity of national characteristics (so that they may still be recognized as different nations), will willingly live in peace under the commonly recognized government of God. Every country will therefore be a theocracy and, as Michael Green puts it, 'the nations of the saved will have no desire but to do their Father's will'.[22] Global Godliness! What a prospect and, because of this Godly political unity, for the first time ever there will be national security without the need for secrecy, balanced by national co-operation untainted by self-interest.

Indeed, the sense of the presence of the Lord will be so strongly felt in all corners of the globe that the river of the Lord's love flowing around the earth will serve to keep international relationships in good health. This is surely the meaning of these verses recorded by John:

> Then the angel showed me the river of the water of life, bright as crystal, flowing from the throne of God and of the Lamb through the middle of the street of the city. On either side of the river is the tree of life with its twelve kinds of fruit, producing its fruit each months; and the leaves of the tree are for the healing of the nations.[23]

Michael Wilcock, commenting on these verses, writes, 'With the curse removed by Christ, the new creation will eventually be what it was meant to be: the throne at the centre of all, and the people of God seeing him, serving him, sealed by his name and reigning with him in everlasting day.'[24]

Whatever national and cultural richness may beautify life in the new earth, it will find its focus in the worship of God whose very presence will saturate every expression of national, tribal or cultural difference. The great chorus of international spirits currently worshipping God in the heavenly places, that 'great multitude that no one could count, from every nation, from all tribes and peoples and languages' which John saw in heaven,[25] will one day receive their resurrection bodies and return with Jesus to the new earth. Still retaining the distinctiveness of their nationhood, they will continue to serve and worship God, singing the songs of heaven on the new earth and declaring that 'salvation belongs to our God who is seated on the throne, and to the Lamb!'[26]

Do we not then expect more after death? Certainly we do! In the age to come, when as resurrected beings we stand in our glorious bodies on the new earth, we shall marvel at a more beautiful creation, revel in the pleasure of more fulfilling human relationships, and worship God in a more united world.

NOTES ON CHAPTER 6

1 G C Berkouwer, *The return of Christ*, Wm B Eerdmans Publishing Co (US), p234.

2 Marie Luise Kaschnitz, 'Life after death', quoted in *Eternal life*, Hans Kung, Collins (HarperCollins Publishers), p182.

3 Millard J Erickson, *Christian theology*, Marshall Pickering, p1234.

4 Genesis 3:15–19.

5 Romans 8:20.

6 Genesis 1:31.

7 Isaiah 65:15–25.

8 John D Watts, *Isaiah*, vol 2, Word Bible Commentary, Word Books, 1987, p357.

9 Alec Motyer, *The prophecy of Isaiah*, Inter-Varsity Press, 1993, p125.

10 Louis Berkhof, *Systematic theology*, Banner of Truth Trust, 1971, p737.

11 Space prevents a full discussion of who will be on the new earth and who will be excluded. Some believe that in the end God will save all humanity (Universalism); some believe that God himself selects only a few for salvation into the new age (Restrictivism); and some believe that a wide range of people will benefit from Jesus' saving work because they have responded to what they know of God in faith (Inclusivism). Restrictivists and Inclusivists therefore both believe (though for different reasons) that some will be excluded from the new earth having walked the 'broad road that leads to destruction' rather than the narrow road that leads to life. Universalists believe that somewhere over the horizon both roads merge. For a fuller examination of these views see *No other name* by John Sanders, Wm B Eerdmans Publishing Co (US), 1992.

12 Matthew 22:30.

13 Stephen Travis, *I believe in the second coming of Jesus*, Hodder & Stoughton, 1988, p173.

14   Luke 20:34–36.
15   Ben Witherington III, *Jesus, Paul and the end of the world*, Paternoster Press, 1992, p218.
16   Anthony A Hoekema, *The Bible and the future*, Paternoster Press, 1979, p252.
17   Walter Rauschenbusch, *A theology for the social gospel*, Macmillan, quoted in *I believe in the Second Coming of Jesus*, see above, p235.
18   Gordon Wenham, *Genesis*, Word Bible Commentary, Word Books; see also Genesis 11:1–9.
19   Zephaniah 3:9.
20   1 Corinthians 13:1.
21   Micah 4:1–4.
22   Michael Green, *The second epistle of Peter and Jude*, Tyndale New Testament Commentaries, Inter-Varsity Press, 1987, p155.
23   Revelation 22:1,2.
24   Michael Wilcock, *The message of Revelation*, The Bible Speaks Today series, Inter-Varsity Press, 1991, p212.
25   Revelation 7:9.
26   Revelation 7:10.

Chapter 7

IT'S LIFE, FOLKS, BUT

NOT AS WE KNOW IT

As we continue to indulge ourselves in this biblically informed speculation about our future life on God's re-created earth, we shall look at five other aspects of our life there, namely:

1 Will there be animals?
2 Will we eat and drink?
3 What will worship be like?
4 Will we work?
5 What will it mean to receive 'rewards' in the age to come?

THE ANIMAL KINGDOM

Many of the Old Testament prophets used pictures of an untypical peace in the animal kingdom to typify the tranquillity of life in the age to come. Isaiah wrote:

> Wolves and sheep will live together in peace, and
>   leopards will lie down with young goats.
> Calves and lion cubs will feed together . . .
> Cows and bears will eat together, and their calves and
>   cubs will lie down in peace.
> Lions will eat straw as cattle do.[1]

Some would argue that this wonderfully vivid imagery is just that, a picture or symbol of the peace of the future which tells us nothing of substance about life on the new earth. I beg to differ since there is no reason to suppose that the world to come will not have an animal kingdom. I believe that the weight of biblical evidence supports the view that resurrected humans will live in peace with animals of all sorts and sizes.

Animals were not an afterthought in God's creation. He created them because they brought him pleasure.[2] There is no reason to believe that the pleasure God took in the animals he created has diminished with the passing of time. God loves the animal kingdom so much that not even a sparrow falls to the ground without his noting its passing.[3] God watches over the animal world with such keen interest that he knows when the mountain goats give birth and when the deer calve. It was he who decreed that the ostrich should be stupid(!); he who gave horses their strength; he who teaches the hawk to fly; he who instructs the eagle in the art of nest building and who loves to feed the birds.[4]

Animals are an integral part of God's good earth and (according to the prophets anyway) they will be an integral part of the new earth. Indeed, to believe that this earth could be renewed without an animal kingdom does not do justice to the word 'renew'. An earth without animals would be a completely different sort of earth, not a renewed version of this one. Whether or not the animals in the new earth will be those who have lived on this earth I do not know. It seems unlikely to me that particular animals will be resurrected. This would require us to believe that animals have a spirit which lives on past death in the same way the human spirit does, a spirit that will one day find its completeness in being rejoined to a new animal body. Since the Bible does not indicate that animals have an eternal spirit within them, and they do not feature in biblical glimpses into the spiritual heavenly 'waiting room' of Paradise, it is perhaps safer to picture a huge new act of creation in which another animal kingdom is brought into being, an animal kingdom which will look like this one but is not this one resurrected. So there will (perhaps) be black collies on the new earth, but I do not expect to find the one that I currently own bouncing up to me wanting to chase sticks!

Whatever the case, we may be certain that the re-created animal kingdom will be at perfect peace with itself and with humankind. We will not hunt animals nor they us and, most incredibly, since all animals will be herbivores and 'eat straw as cattle do' they will not be a threat to one another.[5]

This may sound too fantastic, but it is merely a return to God's original, pre-Fall plan for the animal creation. Alec Motyer, commenting on these verses, says, 'There is a change in the very order of things; the herbivoral nature of all the creatures points to Eden restored.'[6]

In the beginning (before the Fall) God said, 'To every beast of the earth, and to every bird of the air, and to everything that creeps on the earth, everything that has the breath of life, I have given every green plant for food.'[7] In the new earth, where death is one of the former things that will not be remembered, God will once again create an animal world which is satisfied with grass, hay and straw and which therefore can live in peace with itself.

FOOD FOR THOUGHT

All this talk of food perhaps makes us wonder whether humans will eat in the new earth. Although eating is a very important and pleasurable part of our human experience now, some would contend that in the age to come our new bodies will not need 'fuel' and that the 'physical' pleasure of eating will no longer mean anything to us. This view has doubtlessly been reinforced by the 'spiritual' view of heaven and our future that has been so widespread in the church. After all, where *would* a spirit digest its spaghetti?

The argument for a food-free future is given biblical teeth (albeit, as we shall see, false ones!) by some commentators, who appeal to Paul's first letter to the Corinthians for proof. Paul wrote, ' "Food is meant for the stomach and the stomach for food", and God will destroy both one and the other.'[8] Anthony Hoekema concludes, 'According to this passage, the digestive functions of the body will no longer be necessary in the life to come.'[9] And Millard J Erickson, marrying Hoekema's view with Jesus' teaching about the absence of marriage, asks, 'If there is to be no eating nor sex, will there be any pleasure in heaven?'[10]

However, before jumping to these conclusions we must ask whether it was Paul's purpose here to teach about eating in the age to come. Remember that Paul was writing to the Corinthian church which had become obsessed with 'spiritual' things and dismissive of 'physical' things. The Corinthians argued that, since God was really only interested in the welfare of their *spirits*, what they did with their *bodies* was irrelevant. They could eat what they liked since their stomach was of little importance to God and would be destroyed at death, and they could have sexual relationships with who they liked for much the same reason.[11]

Paul, in combatting this sub-Christian over-spiritualization of God's interest in life, points out that whereas the body will indeed be destroyed at death, it still belongs to the Lord and will one day be 'raised by his power'. He counters their extreme libertarianism by reminding them that their bodies, far from being bound for destruction, are bound for resurrection. In other words, Paul is arguing that the body is of great interest to God; it belongs to him and he plans not to discard it but to resurrect it. Since physical resurrection of the body is God's intention and since our bodies even in this age belong to him, we should, maintains Paul, 'glorify God in our body'.

These verses cannot then be used to substantiate a spiritual, stomachless future existence since that is almost the exact opposite of what Paul is teaching in the context of the letter! He wants the Corinthians to realize that, though their bodies (including their stomachs!) will certainly die, God's future intention of physical resurrection gives heightened status to physical life now; since God wants us to have bodies now and in the future, we should see them as sacred and treat them accordingly! There is no good reason based on this passage to suppose that in the age to come we shall have a purely spiritual existence, deprived of the pleasures of food and drink.

Positively, we should note that many of the Old Testament prophecies and some of the New Testament ones mention eating and drinking in the age to come. For example, Isaiah foresees the day when God's people will 'build houses and dwell in them; they will plant vineyards and eat their fruit'.[12] Jesus told his disciples that he would never again drink wine until 'that day when I will drink it new in the kingdom of God'.[13] William Lane comments, 'There is here a clear anticipation of the messianic banquet when the Passover fellowship with his followers will be renewed in the Kingdom of God.'[14]

The age to come was frequently pictured as a feast or banquet[15] and, whilst these references to eating and drinking with Jesus doubtlessly symbolize a richness of end-time fellowship with him, there is no reason to presume that they do not also foreshadow a literal eating and drinking together.

If we shall eat (and there appears to be no biblical reason to doubt that we shall) we, like the animals, will revert to pre-Fall vegetarianism. In creation mankind was given permission to eat 'every plant yielding seed that is upon the face of the earth, and every tree with seed in its fruit'.[16] It was only after the Fall and the coming of death into God's created order that, when Noah left the ark, God said, 'Every moving thing that lives shall be food for you; and just as I gave you the green plants, I give you everything'.[17] (I sometimes wonder what would have made it off the ark if God had given Noah permission to eat meat *before* they set sail rather than *after*!) In the re-creation, with no dead meat to finish up, mankind will presumably be fulfilled in planting vineyards and drinking their wine, making gardens and eating their fruit.[18]

So, will we eat and drink in the age to come? Yes, I believe so. We will also enjoy producing the plants and fruit which we shall eat. The act of eating and drinking will be a pleasure, an occasion for fellowship with others, and an edible reminder of our fellowship with the Lord whose new earth has proved to be so fruitful for us. In that sense every meal on the new earth will be a messianic banquet!

WORSHIP AS A WAY OF LIFE

At this moment in time if we could only share John's experience and peep behind heaven's door (heaven in the true invisible-half-of-present-reality sense!) we would, like him, be almost bowled over by the intensity of music making in worship of the Lamb on the throne.

The throne room of heaven is currently populated by beings whose chief end is to glorify God by singing his praises. Spiritual beings of all sorts – angels and the spirits of departed dead – join in great outbursts of praise to Jesus. 'You are worthy,' they cry, 'to receive power and wealth and wisdom and might and honour and glory and blessing.'[19] This mighty vocal waterfall of praise is doubtless a response to the closeness of the Lamb. Those in heaven now, who see him as he is, cannot help but worship in reverence and awe.

We may, if we die before Jesus returns, be privileged to join in that great heavenly multitude that 'no one [can] count, from every nation, from all tribes and peoples and languages' standing before the throne and crying out in a loud voice, 'Salvation belongs to our God who is seated on the throne and to the Lamb'.[20] But that is a description of heaven (properly understood), not a description of the new earth. However, the time will come when this heaven and this earth 'pass away' and the new heavens and earth are revealed.[21] What will it mean to worship in a resurrected body on the new earth?

One of the most amazing promises regarding the new earth is to be found in Revelation 21:3. It doesn't concern the nature of the earth itself, nor the nature of our resurrected life, but the nature of God's involvement with his new re-creation. In his vision John hears 'a loud voice speaking from the throne: "Now God's home is with human beings! He will live with them, and they shall be his people. God himself will be with them . . ."' (Good News Bible).

In first century Judea Jesus, the Son of God, 'emptied himself' and was 'born in human likeness'.[22] God in human form, living in his creation as part of it. Amazing! Small wonder that those who understood his true identity in those days fell down and worshipped him.[23]

After thirty-three years of life on earth Jesus, resurrected from the dead, returned to his Father (his resurrection body apparently as capable of entering heaven as enjoying the physical pleasures of earth). On his return to the Father, Jesus fulfilled his promise and sent the Holy Spirit of God to indwell faithful human beings. God taking residence in the earth in human beings! Small wonder that those who are filled with his Spirit cry out, 'Abba! Father!' in worship and awe.[24]

At the end of the age Jesus has promised to return to the earth to judge all things and to herald the renewal of all things. With evil finally destroyed and the earth renewed something wonderful happens – wonderful beyond comprehension or description. The Father joins the Son and Spirit on earth. 'Now God's home is with human beings! He will live with them . . .'[25] God's home (heaven) will become enmeshed with our home (earth) so that his presence becomes almost tangible in everything.

Now if the presence of the Son in first century Judea inspired worship in those close to him, and if the presence of the Spirit in this 'pentecostal' age inspires worship in those in whom he lives, what will the presence of the Trinity in its entirety mean? Surely his all-pervading presence will inspire a constant attitude of worship, awe, thankfulness and praise in every one of the redeemed, wherever they live on the new planet.

> Here in this world and amidst the things of time our real-ization of the presence of God is spasmodic; but in [the age to come] we will be permanently aware of that presence . . . In the new age the glory of God is not to be a transitory thing, but something that abides permanently with his people (William Barclay).[26]

Every act will be invested with Godly significance. Like Brother Lawrence we shall not only practise but *experience* the presence of Christ in all the details of our lives. This is perhaps what the prophet Zechariah foresaw when he wrote, 'On that day there shall be inscribed on the bells of the horses, "Holy to the Lord." And the cooking pots in the house of the Lord shall be as holy as the bowls in front of the altar; and every cooking pot in Jerusalem and Judah shall be sacred to the Lord of hosts . . .'[27] In other words, whatever we see, touch or use will somehow point us to the one who made it for us since his presence will be inescapable.

Worship will thus become a normal part of life, not a separate 'spiritual' activity. Wherever we are, whatever we are doing and whoever we are with, it will not be odd for us to fall on our face before our Maker in praise and adoration. 'No one will be self-conscious . . . There will be no competition, no wandering thoughts, no conflicting ideas [about how it should be done]. We will worship by the Spirit perfectly' (R T Kendall).[28]

Indeed, in some small way perhaps we already experience this spontaneous urge to worship our Father in the here and now. Certainly worship even in this age should be an experience which touches all of life, not just our church services (or 'times of worship'). This was the experience of the newly converted A W Tozer.

> I became a Christian when I was a young man working in one of the tyre factories in Akron, Ohio. I remember my work there. I remember my worship there too. I had plenty of worshipful tears in my eyes. No one ever asked me about them, but I would not have hesitated to explain them.
>
> You can learn to use certain skills, until they are automatic. I became so skilful that I could do my work, and then I could worship God even while my hands were busy.[29]

Worshipping God even while our hands are busy with the business of life on the new earth will be our experience. Every duty will be for God and inspire praise. Every relationship will be founded on God and generate thankfulness to the Father.

Every breath will remind us of the Life Giver and will inspire worship. Society will be a worshipping society, not in the sense that all we will do is sing songs in harp-accompanied four-part harmony, but in the sense that every part of life will be touched by God and draw a response from us. Life will be worship and worship will be life.

WORK ON THE NEW EARTH

Apart from eating, worshipping and relating to others, what else will there be to do on the new earth? Some would say, 'Nothing', since we will be perfect and the earth will be perfect. You cannot do anything to improve perfection, so what point will there be in doing anything at all?! Presumably the same question could have been asked by Adam and Eve in the garden of Eden, set as perfect human beings in God's perfect new creation . . .

However, despite the fact that God had created a 'very good' earth for them to live on, he apparently had plenty of ideas of how they could work on it a bit more! The earth was 'perfect', in one sense, but it was clearly not 'complete' since it still required mankind to 'subdue it' and 'have dominion' over it.[30] Creation was not a fixed state but a huge, finely balanced organism, full of rich resources to be discovered and developed.

Humans themselves – although created 'very good' – had potential that would only be fulfilled by the passing of time and the assimilation of experience. 'Part of God's plan for the earth is that it be filled and subdued by humankind, that its latent possibilities be unlocked and actualized in human history and civilization' (Albert Wolters).[31]

Over the millennia, and despite the crippling effects of the Fall, mankind has been able to fulfil this 'creation mandate'. Humankind, often without acknowledging its Creator at all, has used its God-given intellect and creativity to discover and harness much of the potential that God placed in his creation. The silicon chip, penicillin, principles of flight, natural fuels . . . The list could go on and on. The treasure house of the earth has slowly been unlocked and its resources used – sometimes for good and sometimes for ill. The Bible starts in a garden and ends in a city, and maybe this in itself is a symbol of humanity's achievement in developing God's earth.

However, all of this is now in *this* earth. The question remains, will we need to steward the new earth in the same way we have been stewarding this one? Will the progress made on this earth in this present age be lost or retained? On planet New Earth will we revert back to primitive mankind in the garden state, or will we be resurrected as modern mankind in the city state?

First, there is no reason to suppose that the perfection of the new earth excludes development. 'Christian hope is holy expectation, and there will never come a time when that hope will die, for were that possible, much of "heaven" would go. But in our progress there, new vistas of wonder will be ever opening up, new glories of our inheritance will for ever be revealed, new heights of attainment ever be disclosed' (W Graham Scroggie).[32]

It may well be that, like Adam and Eve, we are commissioned to steward and develop the new earth. A new world of resources to discover and harness. New vistas of beauty to capture in paintings, poetry and song. Every new discovery the occasion of a great outburst of praise and worship to the one who revealed it and created it. This kind of new earth is exciting and far from traditional views of 'heaven' that have led many Christians to wonder whether they will enjoy eternity once the first flush of relief at getting there has passed! J B Priestley comments, 'People who do think they are going there often wonder what they will do with themselves in heaven. They make the mistake of assuming that the place will be all complete, finished to the last bit of gilding when they get there. But of course it won't!'[33]

To be sure, there will have to be redeployment on a massive scale. Policemen, doctors and nurses, evangelists, undertakers, locksmiths, burglar-alarm salesmen, bank managers and debt-collectors (along with many others) will all need retraining for gainful employment on the new earth! But everyone will have a role in stewarding the re-creation and everyone will be perfectly suited to that role, finding complete and utter fulfilment in their labours. No longer will work be under a curse so that we have to work hard and sweat to produce anything of worth.[34] The results of the Fall will be remembered no more! Work itself will have been redeemed!

So if work will be a joyful part of the expression of our lives on the new earth, let us think about the second question. Will all that has been achieved in centuries of human achievement be lost in the fire of judgement? Will God wipe out all progress in science, technology and the arts, or could it be that this very progress will itself be redeemed and granted a place in the new earth?

Surely it is a very narrow view of God's involvement in his world which maintains that all he is interested in is the salvation of our souls. We have seen that God is the God of all creation. We noted at the outset that the earth was not just a disposable space-station on which God could work his salvation mission, but it was – and still is – his creation and at every step of its development he has been sustaining it. I am sure that many great works of art, architecture and music, along with scientific discoveries and technological advances have delighted God. Certainly he may not approve of all human creative effort (that which degrades what is good or glorifies evil, for example), nor will he be pleased with some of the applications to which otherwise 'good' discoveries have been put (such as medical advances which have facilitated abortion). But it is unthinkable that God should judge all the progress made (by his enabling) through human endeavour worthless – as deserving to be burnt with judgemental fire.

Surely the finest and most liberating achievements of the ages, those aspects of human endeavour that have been in harmony with God's desire for his world, will be retained and assimilated into life on the new earth. Abraham Kuyper, the Dutch evangelical theologian, writes, 'If an endless field of human knowledge and of human ability is now being formed by all that takes place in order to make the visible world and material nature subject to us, and if we know that this dominion of ours over nature will be completed in eternity, we may conclude that the knowledge and dominion we have gained over nature here can and will be of significance, even in the kingdom of glory.'[35] What a wonderful thought. In the economy of God not a scrap of worthwhile effort will be wasted. Efforts made to extend his kingdom in the sphere of human endeavour in this age will have significance for life in the age to come. This surely gives incentive to achieve ever greater things for God in all areas of life.

Michael Wilcock sums up this hope well when he says, 'All that is truly good and beautiful in this world will reappear there [in the age to come], purified and enhanced in the perfect setting its Maker intended for it; nothing of real value is lost.'[36] Hallelujah!

NO TIME TO LOSE?

As a footnote to this line of thinking, some have observed that since eternity will be 'timeless' the idea of development, or the progressive realization of potential, is meaningless. If there is no 'future', there is no point in setting to work 'today' to create something to be enjoyed 'tomorrow'! Once again we must ask whether this view is watertight. Will there be a sense of time passing in heaven?

There seems no good biblical reason for supposing that time will be abolished. Indeed, if we are convinced that it is God's intention to renew *all* things, why should we imagine that time, which is quite clearly a part of this creation, will not be re-created as a part of the next?

In the Buddhist 'Nirvana' time is done away, but it is not as definite as that in the Christian 'heaven' [ie the age to come]. There are a number of roadblocks barring the way to that conclusion. There is no clear statement of Scripture that in the age to come there will no longer be time or duration. It would be difficult to imagine, for example, how there could be singing in 'heaven', or harp-playing, were there no such thing as time. Music without a beat? A new song without time? (J Oswald Sanders).[37]

What it will mean to have time without the limitations and pressures inherent in 'time' for us today is difficult to imagine. Much illness today is stress-related and stress has been called 'hurry-sickness'. Will it not be incredibly wonderful to experience all the fulfilment of human life without the constant strain of hurrying to be on time or to meet deadlines, to know the pleasure of passing time with people or in a certain pursuit without the pressure of time causing stress and worry?

There may well be a sense of 'just now' or 'in a moment', and the prospect of time passing need in no way detract from any of the glorious hope and security of our eternal state.

REWARDS

No attempted glimpse into the future of life on planet New Earth would be complete without returning to the notion of rewards. In chapter two we noted that Jesus promised to return to earth to reward the faithful, and in chapter three we reflected on heaven as being the 'place' where God 'stores' the rewards until it is time for their distribution.

Donald Guthrie sums up the Bible's teaching about rewards in five concise statements:

1 God will give rewards on the basis of what has been done in this life.
2 The rewards are partially received here but mostly reserved in heaven.
3 The final rewards will be gained on the Day of Judgement.
4 The rewards are of a 'spiritual' nature, like 'the crown of righteousness', but their character is not otherwise specified.
5 There is no suggestion that salvation itself comes under the category of a reward.[38]

Something within us is uneasy with the notion of different rewards in the new earth for faithful Christian service given in this age; it smacks of inequality, even of favouritism. However, when thinking of these God-given service awards, we should remember that they do not equate to our salvation which will be freely and equally given to all who deserve it. No Christian will be any more or less saved than any other on that great day since salvation is a free gift to the faithful not a reward to be earned. Further, in a future world where jealousy, selfish ambition and resentment are presumably amongst the sinful things that are 'remembered no more' the rewards will not be the cause of envy, divisiveness or boasting.

The New Testament often talks about these rewards in terms of crowns, but it is unlikely that we shall participate in the work and worship of heaven staggering under the weight of various sizes of diamond-encrusted headgear! Crowns are surely symbols of God's blessing on our life to come. 'Believers' rewards are not something you wear on your head like a crown ... Your reward ... will be your capacity for service in [the age to come]' (John MacArthur).[39]

Heaven's crowns thus understood represent different levels of appreciation of the age to come. Maybe a person who has a relatively small reward will have only a relatively small capacity to appreciate life on the eternal new earth. He will not feel anything less than totally fulfilled in that nor will others look down on him for being so. Those who inherit a large reward for works done in the here and now will experience eternal life at a much fuller level. They too will be completely fulfilled and will not feel that their reward in any way makes them superior to those around them. Each will be content with their lot.

The following illustration may be helpful. Picture a classical music concert. In the audience there are three very different people sitting next to each other. A middle-aged woman taps her foot to the music, enjoying the tunes and the general sense of occasion. Next to her a keen amateur flautist listens avidly to every note of the orchestra's woodwind section, thrilled at their virtuosity. Next to the amateur flautist a post-graduate music student carefully follows the performance in his own personal music score, noting various nuances in the conductor's interpretation and enjoying the structure that the composer has given to the music.

The middle-aged lady, the amateur flautist and the music student are all experiencing the same performance. Each is experiencing it at a completely different level yet each is content with their ability to enjoy the concert, and each goes home feeling fulfilled by a pleasant evening out.

Maybe this will be a little like our lot on the new earth. All will enjoy the future but some will have the reward of a capacity to enjoy it at a deeper level than others. The promise of reward therefore motivates us to 'give our utmost for his highest' in this age so that we enter the new earth with as large a capacity for appreciating its beauty, realizing its potential and worshipping its Maker as possible.

NOTES ON CHAPTER 7

1 Isaiah 11:6–8 (Good News Bible).
2 Genesis 1:20–24.
3 Matthew 10:29.
4 Job 39:1,13,19,26,27; Matthew 6:26.
5 Isaiah 11:6–8.
6 Alec Motyer, *The prophecy of Isaiah*, Inter-Varsity Press, 1993, p124.
7 Genesis 1:30.
8 1 Corinthians 6:13.
9 Anthony A Hoekema, *The Bible and the future*, Paternoster Press, 1979, p252.
10 Millard J Erickson, *Christian theology*, Marshall Pickering, p1232.
11 See 1 Corinthians 6:13b–20.
12 Isaiah 65:21 (NIV).
13 Mark 14:25.
14 William Lane, *The Gospel of Mark*, New International

Commentaries on the New Testament, Wm B Eerdmans Publishing Co (US), 1974, p508.

15 Eg Matthew 22:1–14.

16 Genesis 1:29.

17 Genesis 9:2,3.

18 Amos 9:14.

19 Revelation 5:12.

20 Revelation 7:9,10.

21 Revelation 21:1.

22 Philippians 2:7.

23 Matthew 14:33.

24 Romans 8:15.

25 Revelation 21:3 (Good News Bible).

26 William Barclay, *Revelation*, vol 2, Canterbury Press.

27 Zechariah 14:20.

28 R T Kendall, *Worshipping God*, Hodder & Stoughton, 1989, p221.

29 A W Tozer, *Whatever happened to worship?*, Kingsway, p98.

30 Genesis 1:28.

31 Albert Wolters, *Creation regained*, Inter-Varsity Press, p63.

32 W Graham Scroggie, from *What about heaven?*, quoted in *Heaven – better by far*, J Oswald Sanders, Highland Books, 1993, p70.

33 J B Priestley, quoted in *God – what the critics say*, ed. Martin Wroe, Hodder & Stoughton.

34 Genesis 3:19.

35 Abraham Kuyper, quoted in *The Bible and the future*, see above, p286.

36 Michael Wilcock, *The message of Revelation*, The Bible Speaks Today series, Inter-Varsity Press, 1991, p211.

37 J Oswald Sanders, *Heaven – better by far*, see above, p90.

38 Donald Guthrie, *New Testament theology*, Inter-Varsity Press, 1981, p862.

39 John MacArthur, quoted in *Heaven – better by far*, see above, p80.

Chapter 8

THREE VISIONARY TALES

I hope, reader, that you will pardon a slight digression in style for this chapter. In the following 'Three Visionary Tales' I have permitted myself the luxury of day-dreaming about what life on the new earth may actually be like. I cannot offer you chapter and verse for every twist of each tale, but I hope that you will recognize many strands of teaching from earlier chapters woven together in these three short stories.

GEORGE'S TALE

It had all happened so quickly that now no one could decide with any degree of certainty exactly what had taken place. Stories circulated of a smoky darkness penetrated by lightning flashes so bright and frequent that night had turned to day, of earthquakes so powerful that it seemed as though nothing could remain standing, and of a gale – a terrible relentless gale – that seemed to sweep away what the earthquake pulled down. Others, whilst unable to remember any of these phenomena, could quite clearly recall an experience within themselves, a kind of burning fire purging the very core of their being. Others again, still rendered half-insensible by the experience, spoke wistfully of the sudden overwhelming presence of Jesus himself, greeting them in a tone so friendly and welcoming that the very act of hearing him had been a form of healing.

To be honest, none of these people could really describe, much less explain, what had happened; they just knew that, whatever it was, they were different now – that everything was different now. Memories of 'the life that was' were already becoming distant. It was consequently difficult to contrast 'the life that was' with this one in any detail, but as George surveyed the scene before him he knew deep inside that this was not how life had always been.

From his vantage point, perched on the parapet of the bridge over the river, he watched a group of men and women cavorting with sheer unrestrained happiness. Staccato snatches of conversation carried to his ears 'Never thought I'd see you again . . .' 'Missed you so much . . .' 'Make up for those lost years . . .'

Separated by he knew not what, George watched their delighted reunion as each took it in turns to hug, laugh and dance with the other. Their joy was punctuated by shouts of 'Thank you, Jesus' and 'Praise the Maker', their ordinary conversation and their worship blending into one natural flow of communication.

George, caught up in the sheer exuberance of their merry making, found himself laughing as he turned to look at another group further away though somehow seeming just as close. This group were standing silently, as still as statues, arms around one another's shoulders, not speaking, totally absorbed in being bound together. One was black-skinned, another white; one wearing the habit of a Catholic nun was held tightly by another wearing the skull cap of a Jew. Completing the circle was a Palestinian woman who, it seemed to George, held onto the Jew with a deeply felt tenderness. This knot of people in their silent unity spoke as eloquently as the first group had done in their hilarity. It was as if the very act of hugging and holding was healing something, reuniting something that had been fractured. None of them could say what it was; they just knew that to stand thus was in itself an important expression of who they had become and why they were there.

The sight was so beautiful that George had difficulty in looking away. But, out of the corner of his eye, his attention was drawn to two familiar figures coming along the road. He looked, and looked again. Yes, there was no doubt. The woman on the right was Diane, his wife in 'the life that was'. He jumped from the bridge and started along the road to greet her.

George had always thought Diane attractive but now, in the Light, she seemed to be more beautiful than ever. As he walked towards her he became more aware of the man walking at her side, a man George had never seen before yet whom, strangely, he instantly recognized as his son, Michael.

The sight of Michael caused George to pause, confused and overwhelmed. What had happened? Michael had been born in 'the life that was' with a disability which had meant that Diane had to carry him everywhere. His legs had been crooked and incapable of bearing his weight, and he had suffered from a breathing disorder which made even the least exertion totally exhausting. George still remembered (although even this strongest of memories was fading fast) how Diane's life had been totally dedicated to carrying him, washing him, feeding him. He could do nothing for himself and had not lived past the age of 10. Now here he was, a strong adult, holding his mother so tightly that he was almost carrying her!

They were both so wrapped up in each other's company that they didn't at first see George, but as soon as they became aware he was there Michael ran to him and threw himself into his arms. Diane joined them in the embrace which, like the hugs of the silent group that George had just been watching, seemed to right a world of wrongs and, at one and the same time, mark both the end and the beginning of an era.

HAROLD'S TALE

Harold pushed his peaked cap back on his head and stared at the root in his hand. 'Amazing. Never seen anything like it,' he muttered to himself in astonished delight. He stood in the garden plot, fork in one hand and in the other the largest, most perfectly formed carrot he had ever pulled from the ground. 'Hallelujah. Thank you, Father,' he said as he bent to pull some more from the neat row that he had sowed last month . . . or was it last year . . . or yesterday even? He could not remember, but anyway it was irrelevant. Here was just one more delight in a sea of endless delight.

Discovery had piled upon discovery for Harold working his garden in this Saved New World. The soil yielded to the fork as though it was co-operating in its own cultivation. No weeds or pests appeared to blight the growth of his crops and the seeds that he sowed sprang up quickly and uniformly, cropping so heavily that he seemed to harvest at least twice as much from each sowing as he had anticipated. There was always more than enough of everything to share with his neighbours and with any stranger who might happen to be passing through the village.

Harold straightened up again and reflected on another delightful discovery – the fact that though he had been bending in the garden all morning, never once had his back ached or his legs felt tired. Day after day he had worked with no hint of boredom or exhaustion marring the experience. His body seemed to be the possessor of infinite strength and powers, so that running, standing or sitting required the same minimal levels of exertion.

He looked across the lawn to where the neighbours were gathered, shelling peas in happy alliance. No one knew whose peas came from which garden but there was plenty for everyone, so no one became anxious that there might not be enough to go around. As they worked, two horses harnessed together ambled around the corner of the barn with Mary who had been using them to mow the grass in the adjacent field.

Humanity had the expertise to replace horses with mechanized machinery for farm work but had reached the decision that it was not right to do so. As yet no one had discovered how to create a fuel which did not pollute the earth and so the widespread use of machinery in all walks of life had been put on hold while more research was done. In any case, the main advantages of using machines were that they would be quicker, save labour and in the long run be cheaper, but in a world where no one was in a hurry, where work was a delight, and where the cost of something was irrelevant since no one charged anyone for anything, cost-effective labour-saving machines had somehow lost their appeal!

Of course there were machines which men and women used to harness the potential of the earth. Wind- or tide-driven generators provided electricity for each community. The power was used to run numerous other machines and engines, such as the pumps carrying water to each town and village and the printing presses in the cities. Every generator was inscribed with the words 'Thanks be to God', and the very hum of each generator somehow sounded a note of praise to the Creator of the winds and tides that drove them.

Freed from their harness, the horses remained near the group. One munched contentedly on the grass round about while the other lay basking in the sun. A hen fussily strutted her way to join them, then a fox slid in and nestled up into the warm strength of the reclining horse's side. The four creatures – the two horses the fox and the hen – seemed to seek and enjoy one another's company and became a symbol for Harold of the way that life was now. Peaceful and harmonious, it was somehow 'right'.

Harold joined his neighbours and sat to share in their task. As he did so, someone spontaneously began to sing a hymn of praise to the God of All The Earth. As each joined in the song the sense of God's presence became so strong that the work of shelling peas had to be put aside for a moment in favour of worshipping the Father and his Son.

At last the chorus ended and the shelling was resumed so naturally that it was almost impossible to say where work had started and worship ended. Although the distant past was beyond his powers of recall, Harold just knew that this was life as it should be. He had never enjoyed his garden so much, never found people so easy to relate to, never seen the world look so beautiful and never felt his beloved Saviour to be so close. Forgotten centuries of waiting were all worth it. Nothing, absolutely nothing could be better than this, he thought.

GABRIELLA'S TALE

Gabriella smiled. It was enough to make anyone smile. Here she was, one of a band of cheerful women moving through the streets of Brazil's capital city. Her memory had begun playing tricks on her so that she was no longer sure of what she thought she remembered, but she was almost certain that she recalled huddling in the doorways of this street as a small child long, long ago in a different world.

Yes, surely that was the very building where she had sat from early morning to late at night, selling flowers she had picked from the gardens of the big houses up the hill before dawn while their owners still slept. It had been dishonest but what was she to do? She had never known her father, and her mother had died prematurely as a result of diseases caught from her 'trade' as an escort to the city's businessmen. Gabriella was on the streets from the age of three, at first under the protection of some twelve-year old girls who showed her where to steal food, where to shelter at night and where to find the flowers to sell from 'her' doorstep.

As time went on Gabriella, at nearly ten, assumed responsibility for some younger children who had been forced to live rough when their parents were murdered by drug-crazed bandits up in the hills beyond the city limits. It was not much of a life but it was all she had, and the needs of her 'little ones' gave her a reason for continuing the daily quest for basic survival. At least the income from flower sales meant that she had not had to sell her body in the same way as her mother; not yet anyway.

Across the street from her doorstep was the Catholic church, and once a week the nuns would come across and invite Gabriella and her little 'family' into the white house behind the church. The big enamel bath would be filled with piping hot water and as soon as they arrived they would strip and wallow in the soapy heaven. After selecting clean clothes from the piles of assorted garments in the corner of the bathroom, they were given a hot meal which they ate awkwardly from a plate using a knife and fork.

After the meal, in a time of secure silence, which was for Gabriella a highlight of the week, the nuns would whisper prayers to Jesus. Gabriella had no idea what they were doing or who this Jesus was, but the reverence with which the nuns spoke when talking to him touched her childish, aching heart. She had nothing and no one in the world, but here in this Jesus she sensed the presence of a friend who was just for her. Someone to call her own.

Back on the doorstep she often found herself praying, quietly under her breath lest her companions thought her mad. Her quiet one-sided conversations grew to mean more and more to her as time passed and, in a way, although she could never have explained it, they gave her the strength to keep going.

This then was the pattern for Gabriella's life until one night in April. It was not a good time of year for the flower trade – the gardens of the big houses were almost bare – and consequently Gabriella had returned to the railway arch where she slept with about twenty other children, hungry and feeling rather dizzy. She had lain down, wrapping herself as best she could in a newspaper gleaned from a rubbish bin near the bus stop, and nodded into sleep when loud, echoing footsteps awoke her. Startled awake she just had time to raise her head when the sound of guns being fired told her what was happening.

Stories of these 'street cleansing' gangs were rife in the places where children gathered. Off-duty policemen, in the pay of local business men who found the presence of ragged children an embarrassment and a hindrance to trade, would scour the streets at night, paying visits to known haunts of street kids and shoot them dead. It was cheaper to hire someone to shoot the children than to clothe, feed and house them so, money being the determining factor for all of life, that was the route they chose. As the bullets sprayed the archway, Gabriella cried out, 'Help me, Jesus.' They were her last words.

Gabriella had no recollection of the bullet that killed her. No recollection of anything really until this. What 'this' was she still did not know but here she was, healthy, strong and very much alive, walking the very streets where she had traded flowers, sheltered in doorways from the rain and – strange though it was to say it – where she had been shot dead.

The same streets, yes, but oh what a difference. No rubbish, no atmosphere of decay and fear. No traffic, no rubbish or anti-government graffiti. No news-stands with their stocks of pornography portraying every conceivable vice and perversion in graphic detail. No one seemed to be in a hurry and everywhere there were knots of people, some just talking together, others singing and some literally dancing with delight.

As she eavesdropped on their conversations the name 'Jesus' seemed to be on everyone's lips. So it was he. Her Jesus had brought all this to be. Her Jesus had brought her here. She smiled. It was enough to make anyone smile.

PART 3

CONTEMPORARY IMPLICATIONS OF BELIEF IN A RENEWED EARTH

'When the expectation of a new earth is denied, the meaning of life on this earth breaks down. Only with an eye to God's future can one understand the richness of life in the present.'

G C Berkouwer

Chapter 9

KNOWING THE END
FROM THE BEGINNING

I hope the contents of this book have made you think afresh about heaven, life after death and your eternal destiny on the new earth as a child of the Father. It would be good to close by asking, what are the implications of this view of the future for our life in the here and now? Is it only vaguely interesting to those of us who like to think about theological issues, or is there something of present-tense, life-enhancing substance here for every Christian?

Theological truth should never be a purely academic thing. The more we understand God and his purposes, the more closely we can relate to him and, with the help of his Spirit, conform our lives to his great eternal plans. So, in conclusion, let us think about some of the contemporary implications of the theology of a new heaven and a renewed earth.

THE NEW EARTH AND THE PRAISE OF ITS MAKER

The creative work of God has always been a great motivation for praising him. Even worship in the heavenly places is, in part, a response to God's creative genius. 'You are worthy, our Lord and God, to receive glory and honour and power, for you created all things, and by your will they exist and were created.'[1] From the perspective of heaven, earth magnifies its creator so that even the angelic beings lavish praise for earth's existence on its Maker.

In creation we see the powerful hand of God. Today, in our desire to celebrate the truth that our Maker is also our 'Daddy' (Abba) there is a tendency to lose sight of God's awesomely powerful majesty as reflected in creation. Jim Packer laments what he describes as the twentieth century's 'God-shrinking trend' which has so eroded the greatness of God as to make him 'no more than a smudge'![2]

If we do give in to this trend and come to see our God as detached and impotent, watching his beloved creation run down from a distant ivory-towered heaven, then the impulse to praise him is likely to be weak indeed. However, if we will only stop and reflect on it, the awe-inspiring nature of creation itself will be enough to blow away such dusty thoughts of a distant God. The evidence of his nature will be seen in the nature of his creation and we will surely be moved to celebrate his power and praise his greatness with renewed ardour.

Furthermore, if in faith we can celebrate the sheer naked power of a Being who at a word can construct this earth to a new evil-free design, who can resurrect departed spirits into new bodies, who can re-create entire species of long-lost animals and whose very presence can illuminate every act of daily living, then we have a God who is worthy of our praise indeed. The hope of creation restored thus inflates our vision of God's greatness and inspires our acts of praise and worship to new heights of appreciation and new depths of gratitude.

THE NEW EARTH AND COPING WITH DISAPPOINTMENT

'Why do bad things happen to good people?' is not only the title of a Christian book but also the cry of many a Christian heart. Why do we suffer? Does the Bible not promise us anything we ask in Jesus' name? Does it not promise that the prayer of faith will save the sick and that the Lord will raise them up? Did Jesus himself not say that even a mustard seed of faith could move mountains?[3] Why then do we experience the frustration of unanswered prayer, unhealed illnesses and faith-resistant hillocks, let alone mountains?

David Cohen, former general director of Scripture Union, frequently used to assert that 'something is not truly biblical unless it reflects the teaching of the whole Bible'. His point was that we are all good at taking texts we like the sound of and tactfully ignoring texts that jar with our way of thinking!

Any texts taken alone and in isolation from other apparently conflicting texts probably will not tell the whole story. To be biblical we must look at the whole Bible. When we do so in search of reasons for our disappointments in prayer and faith conquests, we must look not only at the half of the picture that encourages us to expect great things to happen in Jesus' name, but also at the other half of the picture which the Bible paints of life in this age.

So whilst it is true that Jesus is 'seated . . . in the heavenly places, far above all rule and authority and power and domin- ion, and above every name that is named, not only in this age but also in the age to come',[4] it is also true that 'we do not [yet] see everything subject to him'.[5]

Although we ourselves are already 'new creations',[6] even now 'blessed . . . in Christ with every spiritual blessing in the hea- venly places',[7] nevertheless 'what we will be has not yet been revealed'.[8] In this age the mystery of the gospel 'that was kept secret for long ages . . . is now disclosed'[9] but even so we merely 'see in a mirror, dimly . . . and know only in part'.[10]

Certainly we must pray in faith as Jesus taught us, that God will 'not bring us to the time of trial, but rescue us from the evil one',[11] but even as we do so we are aware that because of the abiding presence of evil in this age we 'will have trouble'.[12]

We could go on, but the point has been made. The presence of the kingdom of God, the work of the Holy Spirit, the prayers and faith of the believer still do not mean that in this age we shall experience all that there is from God for us. This is not to deny the reality of God's power nor to diminish the importance of faith in the believer, but to acknowledge that we live in a fallen world where sin and evil still conspire to warp God's good creation.

This conflict between the effects of the Fall, with which we still struggle, and the benefits of the inbreaking powerful kingdom of God is indeed one of the identifying marks of this 'present evil age'.[13]

> The modern Christian likes to dwell on present blessings rather than future prospects. Modern Christians egg each other on to testify that where once we were blind, deaf, and indeed dead so far as God was concerned, now through Christ we have been brought to life, radically transformed, and blessed with spiritual health. Thank God there is real truth in that. But spiritual health means being holy and whole. To the extent that we fall short of being holy and whole, we are not fully healthy either. We need to realize that the spiritual health we testify to is only partial and relative, a matter of being less sick and less incapacitated now than we were before. Measured by the absolute standard of spiritual health that we see in Jesus Christ, we are all of us no more, just as we are no less, than invalids in the process of being cured'.[14]

We can be certain that a wonderful future is secured for us or, to use imagery from C S Lewis, that this is merely the end of term; the holidays are soon to come![15] This may help us become more content with our lot here. We should certainly be a people who have faith in God's ability to bring to pass in our present experience all that he has promised to do. But alongside that faith for the present, our vision of the new earth will inspire us to be a people of hope for the future. I know that I will never be physically, emotionally or spiritually perfect this side of death, but for me death is not the end and so I do not lose faith in God; his promises and his love are eternal. In my resurrection body on the new earth I will be perfect. No more creaking knees, inferiority complexes or panic attacks that maybe God isn't there after all!

God in his goodness has permitted some of the powers of the age to come to impact life in this present age. Miracles do happen. God does answer prayer. Sick people are healed. God provides enough evidence of what life will be like there to keep me going when faith is at a low ebb. The hope of a glorious new world to come helps me cope with the harsh realities and disappointments of this one.

Paul said 'faith, *hope*, and love' are the abiding Christian characteristics in this age.[16] Let us express our love of God and our faith in him by a life of love for our fellow men and women, but let not faith for the *present* diminish the sustaining reality of our glorious hope for the *future*.

THE NEW EARTH AND COPING WITH CHANGE

In more global terms hope is a vital ingredient in coping with life. In 1970 Alvin Toffler wrote a book called *Future shock* in which he tried to foresee the effects on society of an ever-increasing rate of change. He saw that whereas previous generations had lived in relatively stable societies in which things developed and changed fairly slowly, modern scientific and technological discoveries would mean that life would become a frantic helter-skelter as one change piled upon another towards the end of the (twentieth) century.

He saw a society 'fast fragmenting at the level of values and life styles' without any agreed basis for holding society together. These increasingly rapid changes in beliefs, values and lifestyles would be more than human beings (who do not cope well with change) could handle and he saw that our environment would become so 'ephemeral, unfamiliar and complex as to threaten millions with . . . breakdown'. It was this breakdown that he called 'future shock'.[17]

The society that Toffler (who is not, as far as I know, a Christian) foresaw is with us now. Things that we thought were for ever, such as a job, a marriage, rising house prices, or the Soviet Union (!) have become transient. We buy the latest technology (a DVD player, new generation mobile phone, digital camera) and a new model is produced almost before ours is out of the box. The pace of change is bewildering and destabilizing and many, feeling that they cannot cope with 'the rat race' that it creates, have simply broken down or opted out.

Family breakdown, stress-related illness and suicide rates are all rising in a society that has more leisure time than ever before. Perhaps it is not surprising that people who see this life as all there is get caught up in the flow of life as it happens and, having no other map to guide them than that drawn by contemporary trendsetters, are swept along, failing to notice until too late that the flow is carrying them along the gutter and down the drain!

However, the Christian with a clear(ish!) view of God's eternal purpose for human life on this planet has a different map and a different way of evaluating the relative merits of the seemingly endless lifestyle options given to us. Some elements of change and 'progress', presented as 'vital to life at the end of the twentieth century' we may thus choose to pass by. 'We must call into question the claim of economic, technical and scientific progress to be its own justification. We must be free to evaluate and even reject progress' (Bob Goudzward).[18]

To put it another way, just because we *can* do something or own something does not mean that we *have* to do it or own it. A biblically informed vision of human destiny therefore helps us to decide what is worth accepting and what must be rejected in society's supermarket of change, thus providing godly parameters for sustainable human existence in our society.

THE NEW EARTH AND LIVING JUSTLY

Once I realize that heaven is not just my spirit lying face down before the Lamb on the throne for all eternity, but a resurrected me living in God's redeemed society on God's renewed earth, I have a long-term reference point for my dealings with others. Catching a vision of end-time racial harmony – diversity and difference without prejudice or abuse – will challenge our dealings with people from different cultures in this age. In the kingdom to come 'the unimportant are on centre stage' and 'the ultimately important relationships are utterly astonishing. The last are first, the first are last. The beggars are at the banquet' (Peter Cotterell);[19] this must surely influence who we invite to our 'banquets' in this age. Putting it simply, if we are going to spend eternity relating to someone, we may as well start getting the hang of it now!

We are called to live as people of the future, and once we have been touched by the beautiful prospect of fully redeemed relationships – intimacy without lust, intensity without possessiveness and involvement without domination – then we shall aspire to form our present relationships on such eternal principles. If friendships can be that good, why wait for the new earth?

THE NEW EARTH AND ENJOYING LIFE

Once we realize that this earth is highly prized by God, destined for renewal not destruction, then we can begin to prize it and enjoy it at a deeper level. Unfortunately far too many Christians have been unable to see this truth clearly and in consequence have neglected, or even abused, the good creation that God has given human beings to enjoy. Listen to the words of John Calvin:

> For we must hold, that our mind never rises seriously to desire and aspire after the future, until it has learned to despise the present life . . . For there is no medium between the two things: the earth must either be worthless in our estimation, or keep us enslaved by an intemperate love of it. Therefore if we have any regard to eternity we must carefully strive to disencumber ourselves of these fetters.[20]

One hesitates to disagree with so great a theologian as John Calvin, but is it a simple either/or choice between considering the earth 'worthless' or being 'enslaved' by it? Can we not value the earth as God's children, delighting in the things our Father has given to us? Is there not a middle path in which we engage fully and appreciatively in God's good and beautiful creation, and those aspects of culture which have developed to his glory, remain aware of the effects of the Fall and the danger that the Creator must never be displaced in our affection by aspects of his creation, *but at the same time* desire and aspire after the renewal of all things in the future?

Thankfully, once we gain a biblical perspective on God's intention for ourselves and the planet that he loves, we are freed to delight in the creation that Calvin urges us to despise. With the spurious divide between the 'spiritual' and the 'physical' out of the way, every physical act (except sin!) becomes imbued with new significance. If my eternal destiny is physical, then it is permissible to enjoy with heartfelt thankfulness physical life now. I don't have to feel spiritual when I read my Bible, slightly less spiritual when I eat (after all, we have said grace!) and totally unspiritual when I watch football. All of life has eternal significance. Jewish families, untouched by the Greek way of thinking which exalts the spiritual and devalues the physical, have prayers thanking God for every bodily function – including going to the loo! To some Christians this sounds base, but to a Christian who has taken on board the significance of God's attachment to and involvement in real, physical, down-to-earth human existence, it is like a breath of fresh air.

G C Berkouwer makes the point well when he writes, 'When the expectation of a new earth is denied or relativized, the meaning of life on this earth breaks down, because it exalts the spiritual and mystical to an unbiblical height and denies God's long-term interest in the physical . . . Only with an eye to God's future can one understand the richness of life in the present.'[21]

THE NEW EARTH AND GREEN ISSUES

One day I visited two different publishing houses and at both I was given a cup of coffee. At the first the coffee was delivered in a polystyrene cup, and when I had finished the drink I mindlessly picked holes in the cup before throwing it in the bin. At the second the coffee came in a bone-china cup (with matching saucer). The cup was hand painted and finished with gold-leaf gilding; it was the office's pride and joy, and I was privileged (apparently) to drink from it. When I had finished the coffee, I very carefully set the cup back on its saucer and reverentially placed both well out of harm's way in the middle of the table. I did not, even for a minute, consider picking it to pieces and throwing it in the office bin because I knew it was a highly valued item with its own intrinsic beauty and worth.

Many Christians, because of their lack of understanding about God's long-term interest in this world, think that the earth can be treated like the polystyrene cup. After all, it is disposable, destined for the fire. We can pick holes in it, pollute it and destroy parts of it, and since it is only a transient thing, no one, including God himself, will mind very much.

However, once we come to see the earth more like a piece of gold-edged, highly prized bone china, we are forced to re-examine our methods of living on it. A lot of effort was put into creating it, it has intrinsic beauty and value, and, far from being disposable, it is eternally valued by its creator.

John Stott writes, '[We] believe both that God created the earth, entrusting its care to man, and that he will one day re-create it, when he makes "the new heaven and the new earth". These two doctrines regarding the beginning and the end of history . . . give us a respect for the earth, indeed for the whole material creation, since God both made and will remake it.'[22]

This leads us directly to consider Christian responses to causes taken up by environmentalists and the Greens. Sadly, with their eyes fixed on a spiritual God interested only in spiritual transformation of humanity in preparation for a spiritual future, Christians have abandoned the Creator's masterpiece to the ravages of pollution and a whole range of market-led abuses. How can this be? What blindness has descended on us that we can claim to 'love the Lover', but not 'love what the Lover has made'? (Francis Schaeffer).[23]

Conversely, when the scales of such dualistic thinking drop from our eyes and we see how intimately God is involved in his creation – both past, present and future – we have 'a view of creation which emphasizes the goodness of God's world . . . and it gives us therefore every possible incentive . . . to work for the renewal of God's creation and for justice within God's creation' (Tom Wright).[24]

The horrors created by human abuse and mismanagement of the earth are well documented. According to 'The World Guide 2001/2002' every human being harbours in his or her body about 500 synthetic chemicals that were non-existent before 1920, the three parts per million increase in the atmospheric concentration of carbon dioxide (cause of global warming) in 1998 was the largest ever recorded, increasing water shortages threaten to reduce the global food supply by more than 10 per cent, 500 million people around the globe suffer from an almost total lack of drinking water and half the world's people are medically malnourished.[25]

A concern for all of creation will challenge our 'ostrich' position on ecological matters. Sadly, 'we shall continue to have a worsening ecological crisis until we reject the "Christian" axiom that nature has no reason for existence save to serve man' (Schaeffer).[26] But once we realize that God cares, so must we. Once we allow the harsh truth that the hungry of the world are God's created and loved ones, we shall not eat easily until they are fed. Once we take seriously that the beauty in creation is there because God put it there, we shall not rest easily while mankind rapes her for his own selfish gratification. Once we grasp a vision of creation restored in the new earth, we shall strain after living in such a way now as to see the first-fruits of that restoration in our own time.

> In the biblical story, the creation is seen as innately sacred because God created it. It is pervaded by the presence and the purposes of the living God. Christ became a part of it, and God intends to redeem it. If we choose to embrace the biblical vision of a world made new, therefore, we must also commit ourselves to developing a sense of reverence for all created life. We must be in the forefront of those working for the restoration of the created order (Tom Sine).[27]

At the forefront, yes. No one should be shouting longer or louder about what man is doing to the planet, its people and resources than Christians. What a pity that we so often leave the defence of our Master's creation to others. In a world which is poisoning itself to death, where are the Christian voices raised in protest?

It is a serious matter. In the Old Testament, as we have seen,[28] Israel's destiny was inextricably bound up with her tenancy of the land that God had given her. Indeed the Israelites' moral code and their love of Yahweh were both formed and measured by their respect for all of life, not simply their adherence to religious rituals. They were reminded that 'nothing they could do in, on or with the land is outside the sphere of God's moral inspection. From major issues of the defence of the national territory down to how you prune your fruit trees, every area of life is included'. This 'earthiness' in Israelite religion meant that the way that Israel treated the land was a '"spiritual thermometer" assessing the temperature of their relationship with God and their status as God's redeemed people, since a nation that allowed itself to succumb to the same economic evils as the world around could not function as a light to the nations' (Chris Wright).[29] When God uses the thermometer of care for the environment to measure the health of his redeemed people today, I wonder how healthy he finds us to be?

This is challenging. God counts the passing of a solitary sparrow, yet we who love him allow a whole species to go out of existence without shedding a tear. God is not willing that any should perish, yet we watch thousands starve on our TV sets, knowing that our over-consumption is the major reason why they are under-fed. God created a world of ecological balance and beauty, yet we are happy to live with a consumerist lifestyle which is directly responsible for high levels of pollution destroying that ecological balance. God plans to renew his creation, whilst we continue to connive with its destruction. Surely we should 'repent of extravagance, pollution and wanton destruction . . . and . . . strenuously avoid all wastefulness, not only out of solidarity with the poor but also out of respect for the living environment' in which the Creator delights and at whose abuse the Creator grieves (John Stott).[30]

Our view of creation's future will challenge and hopefully transform our life in that very creation in the present. Never again should we adopt a 'polystyrene cup' attitude to the earth, but rather out of reverence for its Creator and his long-term plans for its renewal, we will handle it with the care that so fragile and beautiful a creation deserves.

NEW EARTH AND HUMAN CREATIVITY

Once we have caught a vision of the *continuity* between life in this age and the life of the age to come, the fact that what we do now can have eternal significance will challenge us to aspire to ever greater achievements for Jesus. Formerly we may have thought along these lines . . .

If all human endeavour in the fields of art and science is going to be destroyed by fire, then why bother overmuch about its creation in the first place? If heaven is going to be a spiritual experience, then physical things like paintings, bridges, books, houses, sculptures and furniture surely have no eternal relevance? Difficult to hang a painting on the ethereal wall of your heavenly mansion, and if you can float across the river why build a bridge? However, once we try to think about a redeemed material future, we can also dare to believe that since 'God is a creative God who affirms the goodness of the world he has made, he will not simply write it off with all its wealth of art and beauty and human inventiveness' (Stephen Travis).[31]

We can only guess at how God might redeem these things, but the prospect of him doing so transforms every field of human endeavour. The breadth of God's eternal plans for human creativity liberates us to think that almost every area of life has that which is redeemable within it. At a prayer time following a concert by Christian reggae musician, Ben Okafor, someone thanked God for giving Ben the vision to 'redeem reggae'. At the time it sounded strange to me. *People* were redeemed, not art forms! But now, with a deeper appreciation of God's present interests and future plans, the redemption of reggae sounds wonderfully consistent with what Christians are called to do in all walks of life.

Let's get architecture redeemed, painting redeemed, technology redeemed and dancing redeemed. Let's bring them back into the pure creative stream of God's love, and let's rejoice in the fact that what is redeemed will have a place in our eternal home.

Far fetched? Not if we see redemption as 'the recovery of creational goodness through the annulment of sin' (Albert Wolters).[32] In other words, our work as Christians is not just to engage in mission to see sin defeated in people's lives, but to work to see sin defeated in people's societies, art forms and cultural expression. 'To conceive of either the Fall or Christ's deliverance as encompassing less than the whole of creation is to compromise the biblical teaching of the radical nature of the Fall and the cosmic scope of redemption.'[33]

I am inspired by a prospect of eternal life on a renewed earth where sin has been defeated in every structure of life. Politics without greed and injustice. Relationships without suspicion and lust. Music of all sorts without self-promoting performers or debasing lyrics. Art without the grotesque. Dance without the provocative. Every aspect of life glorifying the Lord and resulting naturally in praise of the Creator of all life.

So, are there practical implications for a belief in a 'new heavens and a new earth'? Yes. The belief I have about the future affects nearly every part of my life. My work and worship. My ability to rise in hope above my circumstances. My enjoyment of creation and my responsibility for the environment. Everything becomes coloured with different hues when my sights become fixed on the new earth where righteousness is at home, where God himself dwells with his people and where the earth is filled with the knowledge of his glory as the waters cover the sea! Amen. Come, Lord Jesus.

NOTES ON CHAPTER 9

1 Revelation 4:11.
2 J I Packer, *A passion for holiness*, Crossway Books, 1992, p69.
3 John 16:23; James 5:15; Matthew 17:20.

4   Ephesians 1:20–21.
5   Hebrews 2:8 (NIV).
6   2 Corinthians 5:17.
7   Ephesians 1:3.
8   1 John 3:2.
9   Romans 16:25.
10 1 Corinthians 13:12,13.
11 Matthew 6:13.
12 John 16:33 (NIV).
13 Galatians 1:4.
14 *A passion for holiness*, see above, pp40/41.
15 C S Lewis, *The last battle*, Puffin (Penguin Books Limited), p165.
16 1 Corinthians 13:13.
17 Alvin Toffler, *Future shock*, Pan (Macmillan Publishers), p293.
18 Bob Goudzward, from *Idols of our time*, quoted in *The transforming vision*, Walsh & Middleton, Inter-Varsity Press, p152.
19 Peter Cotterell, *Mission and meaninglessness*, SPCK, 1990, p272.
20 John Calvin, *Institutes of religion* 3 IX 1,2.
21 G C Berkouwer, *The return of Christ*, Wm B Eerdmans Publishing Co (US), p230.
22 John Stott, *Issues facing Christians today*, Marshall Morgan & Scott, 1984, p119.
23 Francis Schaeffer, *Pollution and the death of man*, Crossway Books, 1993, p67.
24 N T Wright, Drew lecture, 1993, used with permission.
25 Data from 'The World Guide 2001/2002 – An alternative reference to the countries of our planet' (New International Publications Ltd) 2001, pp22/23.
26 *Pollution and the death of man*, see above, p84.
27 Tom Sine, *Wild hope*, Monarch, p249.
28 See chapter one.
29 Chris J H Wright, *Living as the people of God*, Inter-Varsity Press, p59/61.